James I. Wallace Ph.D.

ON TARGET

Comparative Challenges
of Sports & Games

James I. Wallace Ph.D.

ON TARGET

Comparative Challenges
of Sports & Games

Copyright © 2025 by James I. Wallace Ph.D.

All rights reserved. No part of this publication may be reproduced, distributed, or transmitted in any form or by any means, including photocopying, recording, or other electronic or mechanical methods, without the prior written permission of the copyright owner and the publisher, except in the case of brief quotations embodied in critical reviews and certain other noncommercial uses permitted by copyright law. For permission requests,write to the publisher, addressed "Attention: Permissions Coordinator," at the address below.

CITIOFBOOKS, INC.
3736 Eubank NE Suite A1
Albuquerque, NM 87111-3579
www.citiofbooks.com
Hotline: 1 (877) 389-2759
Fax: 1 (505) 930-7244

Ordering Information:

Quantity sales. Special discounts are available on quantity purchases by corporations, associations, and others. For details, contact the publisher at the address above.

Printed in the United States of America.

ISBN-13:	Softcover	979-8-89391-683-6
	eBook	979-8-89391-684-3

Library of Congress Control Number: 2025909199

Table of Contents

Preface vii

Chapter 1   Competitive Challenges 1
Chapter 2   Major League Sports 7
Chapter 3   Mid-Major Sports 36
Chapter 4   Summer Olympic Sports 44
Chapter 5   Winter Olympic Sports 75
Chapter 6   Less Widespread Sports 83
Chapter 7   Games 97
Chapter 8   The Mental Game 107
Chapter 9   Additional Factors 128
Chapter 10   Discussion 137

References 149
About the Author 153

Preface

• • •

THIS BOOK IS A PERSONAL expression of sports fanaticism. Athletic endeavors make up a vast portion of the fabric of life. Human beings of all ages, in all countries, play and watch sporting events. And since most of such sports are target games, they are hit-or-miss propositions. We score or we don't. We win, lose, or draw. Imperfection often dominates precision. The more arduous the athletic undertaking, the more skill is needed to emerge victorious over that task and one's fellow competitors.

Facts and opinions blend in this volume. One purpose, then, is to convey some interesting information that one may learn about the broad landscape of sports. This book may serve to educate children, adolescents, and young adults about the wide variety and appeal of sports and games—how they are played, what risks and satisfactions they entail, and what makes them attractive. Such knowledge could resonate with youths and spike their interest as viewers or, more importantly, entice them to participate in target games about which they learn here. Popular professional sports are analyzed in considerable detail; less well-known recreational activities are described sufficiently to spark awareness and appreciation of them. Parents, teachers, counselors, and coaches may want to introduce this book to young people to point out to them the benefits to be gained (physical, emotional, moral) by engagement in athletics.

Young and old alike who are already engaged in these games may also profit from reading these perspectives on the sports they embrace. Both high-level athletes and weekend warriors might gain insight, or affirm present practices, from the chapter on sport psychology and performance enhancement—how cognitive and emotional components play into athletic events. Sports fans of all stripes and experience may enjoy learning about facts, trivia, and principles associated with the activities that entertain them. In addition, there is the notion of having fun thinking about, discussing, and debating the relative merits, oddities, complexities, and difficulties of these sporting endeavors. I hope that you'll enjoy reading this.

We will herein take a look at some of the trade-offs, ambiguities, and negative aspects, but this is mainly a celebration of the complicated challenges and satisfactions that athletic competition can bring. Most competitors play to win, but it's admirable and healthy to play sports and games for the sheer enjoyment and benefit of it. Dr. Stuart Brown (2014, p. 5) states it thusly:

> Of all animal species, humans are the biggest players of all. We are built to play and built through play. When we play, we are engaged in the purest expression of our humanity, the truest expression of our individuality. Is it any wonder that often the times we feel most alive, those that make up our best memories, are moments of play?

In the introductory chapter, I define some terms and outline the categories of target games to be explored thereafter. Then it's time for some close examination of the features and challenges of athletic endeavors, starting with the most widespread and popular sports, and then tapering down to some of the strange games that people have created to play. Mental approaches to those sports and games, with an eye toward performance enhancement, is followed by an examination of miscellaneous factors that influence the relative difficulty of certain pastimes. The discussion section tosses around an analysis of which target games pose the biggest challenges, restating one of the main themes of this book. Since this book was originally published in 2016, some athletic rules and records may have changed. After all, sports records are made to be broken.

I would like to acknowledge people who did much to making the writing of this book possible. My father, Louis Wallace, played catch with me with a football and baseball as a child. We played ping pong and basketball, and he was most instrumental in beginning and perpetuating my golf game. Probably more importantly, Dad engaged me in the world of myriad spectator sports and instilled in me the value and perception of fair play. My mother, Anne Wallace, was an all-around athlete. She was powerful yet graceful, skilled and agile. She taught me swimming, diving, water skiing, and alpine skiing, none of which I could ever do with her aplomb. My brother, Larry Wallace, was cut from the same cloth and has shared my involvement in sports, as participant and spectator, over our lifetimes; I value the feedback about this book from him and our cousin, Steve Zaleon. Of course, my wife, Ann Jane Tierney, has been influential, too. She's an athlete, martial artist, and aficionado of exercise who has supported my professional and personal endeavors. Our daughters, Jasmine and Gemma Wallace, are active and inspirational athletes, as well.

There have also been many friends, listed here alphabetically, who played, viewed, and discussed sports with me in strongly influential ways: Albert Ammerman, Gordon Baker, Art Blymiller, Fernando Canales, Peter Fox, Jack Goldsmith, Jim Kofod, Bob Lindstrom, Alex Miner, Jeff Mosher, Ernie Nolen, Mitch Paskin, Andrew Rice, Scott Robinson, John Roginson, Dave Rosenberg, Jonathan Schaller, Joe Share, Andrew Tanner, Russ Wilcox, and Dave Young. I'm grateful to all of them. A special thanks goes to my departed sensei, Rod Kobayashi, for moving me along on the path of aikido and all that has done for my life.

CHAPTER 1

Competitive Challenges

• • •

KEEP YOUR EYE ON THE ball. Be goal-oriented. Focus on the bull's eye. Take dead aim. It's human nature to be attracted to targets. We toss wadded-up paper across a room into a wastebasket. We throw snowballs at trees, telephone poles, signs, and even fellow humans. We throw stones at objects, or try to hit stones with objects. We play catch with friends and family, aiming to connect with the projectile in hand. We shoot bullets, arrows, and other weapons at targets, living or lifeless. We set targets, or goals, for our vocational or everyday endeavors.

This book is about target games and sports. Perhaps darts, rifle or pistol shooting, and archery come readily to mind. Those sports use circular targets that reward aiming at and striking the central bull's eye. Curling, a Winter Olympic but not widely played sport, in some ways more complex than the aforementioned activities because of its interplay with teammates and taking turns with an opposing squad, is another sport with a target of concentric circles. But sports and games need not have such stereotypical targets to be target-oriented. In reality, most of the athletic endeavors we play have targets either explicit or implicit in the action.

People are fascinated by superlatives. What's the best-case scenario or worst-case scenario? Which restaurant is the best in town? What is the worst disaster that has happened? Sports fans are particularly captivated by comparisons among athletes, contests, and eras. Who is the best basketball player now? Ever? Who is the best golfer of all time? Which are the ten worst football stadiums? Who are the top ten quarterbacks? Most of these comparisons presented in the media are within one sport or another, or between two different eras during which the contests have been played. One aspect of this book is the comparison among various sports and games, with little regard for historical context, to debate which might be the most challenging and difficult.

Every sport and game offers its share of challenges. If not for some degree of difficulty, what would be the pleasure of playing and the value of winning? Some sports, like football or rugby, emphasize physical size, strength, speed, and toughness. Games, such as darts or billiards, need finesse rather than power and mobility to execute them well. Both games and sports may prioritize cerebral abilities—to devise and memorize plays, visualize actions, strategize how to overcome opposition, concentrate in the here and now. Epitomizing the union of energies of body and mind, golf blends athletic force with calm eye-hand coordination. Goal-oriented athletes come in all shapes, sizes, and IQs.

We're going to examine a wide variety of activities in some detail in order to see what draws participants and observers, players and fans, to these pastimes. Some sports have small targets—e.g., rifle/pistol shooting target, dart board—while others have expansive targets—e.g., soccer goal, football end zone. Some require only small muscle movements—e.g., shooting pool, pitching tiddlywinks—while others need whole-body coordination—e.g., basketball, hockey. Some are relatively stationary, such as standing/kneeling/lying to aim a rifle, while many require hitting a target on the fly—sometimes with both the thrower (quarterback, point guard) and the target (wide receiver, small forward) in motion simultaneously. Complexities and comparisons are virtually endless. So, too, are the opinions of people who consider one sport or another, perhaps their favorite game, as the most taxing and virtuous athletic activity of all.

This book aims to explore broadly the world of sports, from mainstream to esoteric games, and to address two central questions: (1) Which target games are most challenging, have the highest degree of difficulty? (2) How can we use mental approaches, the lessons of sport psychology, to enhance performance and enjoyment of them? That first topic may lure you, the reader, to ponder where your favorite pastimes rank in the pantheon of athletic task difficulty. The latter topic may be mentioned here and there regarding particular sports, and will be examined in some detail later in this book.

Before target games can be suitably compared, knowing that sports tend to entail more athletic activity than do games, it's a good idea to examine some definitions. According to *Webster's New Universal Unabridged Dictionary*, a <u>game</u> is partially defined as a competitive activity involving skill, chance, or endurance on the part of two or more persons who play according to a set of rules, usually for their own amusement or for that of spectators.

A <u>sport</u> is an athletic activity requiring skill or physical prowess and often of a competitive nature. It may also be a diversion, recreation, or pleasant pastime. <u>Athletic</u>, incidentally, involves the use of physical skills or capabilities such as strength, agility, or stamina. A <u>target</u> is an object, usually marked with concentric circles, to be aimed at in shooting practice or contests. It may be anything fired at or a goal to be reached. Targets include characters in point-and-shoot video games, the goal posts of a football field, home plate, pool table pockets, or the goal of soccer/hockey/lacrosse. More broadly, we may think of a football end zone or golf green. Very specifically, not only must fencers limit their strikes to certain anatomical areas, but so also must amateur boxers and martial arts combatants. Most athletic endeavors, it seems, urge us to hit the center, strike the ball, connect with a teammate, or score points.

We might further classify target games by the following rubric:

- Throw ball at target (bowling, lacrosse)
- Throw/propel other object at target (darts, archery)
- Throw and hit (baseball, cricket)
- Throw and catch (football, lacrosse)
- Hit ball at target (croquet, golf, billiards)
- Hit other object at target (hockey)
- Hit ball past adversary (tennis, racquet sports)
- Kick ball at target (soccer, kickball)
- Target is time (swim, run)
- Target is teammate (football, ultimate Frisbee)
- Target is adversary (boxing, karate)
- Target is distance (javelin, discus, shot put)

- Target to surmount (high jump, pole vault)
- Individual performance (swim, bowl)
- Team performance (basketball, football, hockey)
- Pro vs. amateur sports (NY Giants vs. high school football)
- Interdependent vs. individual sports (basketball vs. golf)

Proponents of various sports, whether players or spectators, probably consider their personal activities to be genuinely high in degree of difficulty. When athletic and recreational activities are being judged for their relative challenge, it helps to explore the factors and complexities endemic to each game. Hereafter, knowing that it's impractical to go into detail about, or even mention, each and every one of the hundreds of sports and games that humans have devised to fill their recreational and/or professional lives, we'll look at some prominent examples. Specific rules and guidelines highlight the tasks at hand, as do statistics regarding play. As we'll see, however, subjectivity likely rules when it comes to comparing the games that appeal to us.

The following selection of target sports and games is likewise subjective. It is not intended to be an exhaustive list of every such activity. I mean no offense if I've omitted the reader's favorite pastime or explored it in relatively less detail. I either lack the experience to discuss those topics in a knowledgeable, analytical manner, or wish to limit this treatment to the games and sports included. I have chosen to classify sports into the categories of major league, mid-major, Summer Olympic, Winter Olympic, less widespread (more esoteric), and games. I've also injected a section about sport psychology to examine how the mind and body interact to enrich the challenge and satisfaction of athletic endeavors. Some direct and tangential facets of athletic competition are outlined, and a discussion section wraps up this book with more data and opinion.

With these generalities in mind, let's begin scanning more specifically the wide world of target games and sports.

CHAPTER 2

Major League Sports

• • •

THESE SPORTS GET CONTESTED IN professional leagues or many major championship tournaments in the United States and, in some cases, around the world. They are played in all divisions of inter-collegiate athletics. They are the subjects of widespread media coverage. Not merely by coincidence, they are clearly target games.

Baseball
Basketball
Football
Golf
Hockey
Soccer
Tennis

BASEBALL
Superficially, the sport of baseball may appear to be a simple endeavor. A batter hits a ball, then runs or trots around the four bases, scoring a run if he makes it all the way to home plate. Ballplayers toss the round, cowhide ball to one another, catching

it with the aid of a glove or mitt. The baseball batter swings a wooden (or aluminum) implement at a ball (his immediate target) with the goal of swatting that sphere toward an expansive target. Baseball fields, opening up from the point of the infield diamond and stretching through the outfield toward the arcing, distant wall or fence, provide large areas (the secondary target) at which to aim. The ultimate objective—a home run—is achieved when the ball is propelled through the air and over the outfield wall. That fence stands a distance of 302-355 feet along the foul poles in major league baseball (MLB) stadiums, and as far as 390-435 feet away in center field. The height of the outfield wall varies from one park to another, most being around 10 feet high; but the "Green Monster" in Fenway Park in Boston extends 37 feet above the outfield. Softball is a variation of baseball, highly similar but typically played in parks of smaller dimensions. To hit the ball out of the park, far enough for a home run, takes a considerable blend of strength, timing, skill, and bat speed. Of course, any hit that is in fair territory—within the boundaries extending from home plate straight out to the distant foul poles—could result in a single, double, triple, or even inside-the-park home run. Thus, baseball batters have ample space within which to aim, with relative levels of success to be attained therein. So, the game of baseball is rather simple in its set-up. However, there are significant complicating factors.

The timing of the batter's swing must fall within certain parameters. A right hander's swinging early at a pitched ball gets his bat to its junction with the ball a bit early and results in a hit that goes left of center, sometimes far enough to reach foul territory. Naturally, swinging somewhat late pushes the ball right of center. The altitude of the swing relative to that of the ball also has a strong bearing on the success or failure to get a hit. The bat is cylindrical. Swinging it slightly below the center of the spherical ball (just under three inches in diameter) results in a glancing blow that elevates the ball to the outfield, into the infield, or even behind the batter. If the bat is swung a bit high relative to the ball, the downward deflection is typically a ground ball that, on rare occasion, may even hit the batter in the foot or bounce behind him. Solid connections between the rounded surfaces of bat and ball are rather low in frequency. So, the task of hitting a baseball squarely and far is not an easy one.

Let's see, are there any other complicating factors? Oh, yeah: Nine opposing team members place themselves strategically throughout the playing field with the intention of catching a fly ball—in either fair or foul territory—or fielding a ground ball efficiently enough to throw it to a base before the batter (now a runner) reaches it. Either way, the batter is out. Even the catcher, positioned behind the batter, can record outs by catching a pop-up behind or near home plate, or fielding a bunt (a short hit achieved by blocking a pitch with a stationary bat) quickly enough to throw the ball to first base before the batter can scoot there. The defensive actions of the opposing team significantly narrow the target areas of the batter. And there is one other substantial obstacle to a batter's success at hitting his target: the pitcher.

Major league, and even some lower-level, pitchers hurl the baseball at speeds of 70, 80, 90, and even 100 miles per hour. The high velocity of a pitch can combine with bat speed to send the ball farther toward the outskirts of a ball park, but that same speed demands quick reaction and impeccable timing by the batter. Furthermore, pitchers have the skill to spin the ball in ways that make it rise or sink, slide left or right, or curve downward either toward or away from the batter. A spinning, dipping, high-speed baseball is truly a moving target. And woe to the batter who does not remain constantly alert to the possibility that the pitcher might hurl the ball far enough off-line to hit him—ouch! The need to be ready instantaneously to take evasive action can cause disruption to a batter's concentration. Any batter who gets hit by a pitch is automatically awarded a position on first base; just hope that the hard-hitting ball has not struck and injured a point of vulnerability such as one's head.

Batters can succeed in hitting the ball and gaining bases at fairly high rates. For a single season, Hugh Duffy hit safely 44% of his turns at bat; since that was way back in 1894, such a high batting average has since become much more difficult to achieve. For his career, the all-time great Ty Cobb finished with a batting average of .367 over the span of 1905-1928—much success over a long time, but in a bygone era. In general, any baseball player who gets a hit one third of the time is being highly successful. Those batting between .250 and .300 are doing just fine. If you hit in the .200-.250 range, you better contribute some ancillary skills (e.g., fielding well, swatting home runs, stealing bases, drawing walks) to your team. And if your batting average is below .200, you better be a pitcher.

All baseball players, more or less, must take the challenge of being batter. In the American League, at present, pitchers are often excused of that duty in favor of a designated hitter; those pitchers get less batting practice for the times they happen to play in the home, and by the rules, of a National League team. Why are pitchers usually the weakest batters, the ones asked to sit out? Well, let's further examine the role of these multi-tasking experts in this target game.

The pitcher throws the ball primarily at a target called the strike zone. It's 60 feet away from the pitcher's mound. Its width is equal to that of home plate (17 inches) and its height the area from a batter's knees to his beltline. Thus, the altitude varies according to the batter's dimensions and stance. A tall batter who tends to stand upright at the plate provides a relatively tall target for the pitcher, while a short batter who tends to squat beside the plate shrinks the strike zone. If the pitcher can throw three pitches through any part of that strike zone and into the catcher's mitt, with the batter either swinging and missing or merely watching the ball go by, he has succeeded in getting the batter out. Yes, of course, it's more complicated than that. The umpire squatting behind the catcher must judge those pitches to be strikes, not balls. Four balls, tossed outside the strike zone and rightfully ignored by the batter, land that hitter on first base. The batter, along the way, may swing at any pitch and tap it into foul territory; provided it's not caught for an out, that swing is counted as a strike. Only the third strike must be "clean"—either ignored or whiffed by the batter. That batter also has the right to swing at any pitch, in or out of the strike zone, resulting in a strike or a hit according to his timing and accuracy.

And there's even more to the complexity of pitching. (No wonder they tend to be the highest-salaried players.) The target is partly determined by the catcher's signals; he and the pitcher use sign language to converse briefly about what type of pitch to throw and where to aim it relative to home plate and the batter. They take into account what they know about the batter's usual tendencies, as well as the present circumstances of the game (e.g., runners on base or not, the score, the inning). Is he trying to fool the batter into swinging at an errant pitch, thereby striking out? Does he want to lure the batter into hitting a ground ball that results in a double play? Maybe the pitcher wants to "brush back" the batter, to make him stop crowding the plate, or entice him to swing at an outside pitch.

The pitcher must be alert to potential base stealers, throwing the ball accurately and swiftly to first base (or elsewhere) to try to pick off a runner or limit the "lead" he takes. That distraction can interfere with a pitcher's concentration on pitching to the batter at the plate. A pitcher must also field bunts, cover first base or home plate when needed, and be prepared to defend himself should a batter swat a ball right back at him (made more challenging because the pitcher often finishes a pitch in an off-balance position).

How on Earth can a pitcher maintain flexible focus? Reading signs from the catcher, sizing up each batter, staying ready to throw to first (or another) base to prevent steals, all the while being at risk of a ball zooming at a dangerous speed right back at him from the hitter's bat—the challenges are impressive. Being a pitcher with runners on base is like being Bruce Lee surrounded by kung fu antagonists. It's akin to Clint Eastwood's facing off against a band of gun-slinging desperados. It's like being a young marketer trying to pitch a novel idea to a boardroom full of company executives. A pitcher, then, must master attentional control. There's actually no such thing as multi-tasking; the human brain and body can legitimately execute only one action at a time, though in rapid succession if necessary. The pitcher must process information, make decisions, and throw with accuracy in confounding situations. Is it any wonder that pitchers, with so many skills to learn and drill, have little time for batting practice and consequently tend to have the lowest batting averages on their teams? Since this book was drafted, incidentally, the National has joined the American League in having a "designated hitter" replace the pitcher at the plate.

As for the pitcher's battery mate, the catcher has a job we may consider to be nearly as demanding as that of the pitcher. He must deeply squat for long periods of time, signal the pitcher suggested pitches, set his mitt as a target for each pitch, see and catch the rapidly incoming pitch (his immediate target) whether or not the batter distracts his vision by swinging at it, bounce up to catch foul balls lofted in his vicinity, throw hard and fast to second base if a runner tries to steal it, and tag a hard-charging runner who is heading for home plate with or without a collision. The catcher and pitcher collaborate to control the pace of the game. Being a catcher is a cerebral role (e.g., knowing the tendencies of batters of opposing teams) as well as a physically demanding one. An air traffic controller at a busy international airport in some ways faces similar challenges.

Batters aim to hit balls at targeted regions of a baseball field. Pitchers aim at the strike zone and vicinity with the goal of whizzing the ball past the hitter. Does any other baseball player focus on a particular target? The fielders, naturally, must keep their eyes on the ball in order to catch it whether it is sailing through space, rolling on the ground toward them, or bouncing haphazardly in their direction. Then, often times, they must be able hurriedly to throw the ball on target to a teammate, sometimes from deep in the outfield. That may be complicated by the need for a split-second decision of where to throw—to home plate to stop a run from scoring, third base to thwart a lead runner, second base to initiate a possible double play, or simply first base in time to keep the batter from reaching it before the ball gets there.

Baseball—a simple game? Hardly. No matter what variety of the sport—from Little League to Babe Ruth, hardball to softball, minor league to major league, males or females on the diamond—the challenges are similar. And this discussion is limited to the target-oriented aspects of the sport. There's a lot more to it if you think about the changing placements of players in the field (to adjust to batter's characteristics and the circumstances of the current game), determination of batting order, in-game decisions (to steal, bunt, change pitchers), choosing to use pinch hitters and pinch runners, dealing with crowd noise and a variety of visual and auditory distractions, etc. Sportscaster Bob Costas described it well: "Baseball is a game of atmosphere and anticipation, punctuated by moments of brilliance and excitement."

BASKETBALL

The sport of basketball is a straightforward target game. The goal is to put the 9-inch ball into a metal circle or hoop that measures 18 inches in diameter and stands 10 feet above the playing surface. One may do so from any distance, close range (slam dunk or lay-up) to many feet away. A shot that goes through the hoop typically earns one's team two points. But one may earn three points instead of merely two for any shot drained from 19.75 feet in a high school or women's NCAA game, 20.5 feet in a women's professional (WNBA) game, 20.75 feet in a men's college game, 22.15 feet in international (e.g., Olympic) competition, or 22-23.75 feet at the men's professional level (the NBA distance varying from closer at the baseline to farther at the top of the key). The last form of scoring is one point for each free throw made—shot without interference from a distance of 15 feet from the basket.

The five players on a basketball court play designated positions and roles. They are specialists in how they place and move themselves, what skills they emphasize (e.g., dribbling, rebounding, passing), and how they interact with their teammates in the flow of the game. Essentially, however, they all aim for that same target and score accordingly. This task may be perceived as easy given that basketball players succeed in putting the ball into the basket a higher proportion of the time per contest than do their counterparts score in other major sports. Of course, it's not entirely simple.

Part of the challenge comes from the fact that players seek to hit the target in the face of intense opposition. An equal number of players from the opposing team strive tenaciously to steal the ball, block one's path, block a shot, distract, disrupt, deflect, and otherwise interfere with one's progress toward the goal. If you fancy yourself a good shooter of a basketball, try doing so against some of the tallest human beings on the planet. Those somewhat less tall may have awesome quickness and/or leaping ability. And elite basketball players tend to be wiry strong, fluidly agile, and as athletically gifted as participants in any sport. They present formidable obstacles to scoring.

Time limits complicate matters. Players have deadlines within which to launch a shot (that at least draws iron—i.e., touches the rim of the basket). The shot clock expires in 30 seconds in men's college games, 30 seconds in women's college games, and 24 seconds in NBA, WNBA, and international competition. (Only seven states currently require a shot clock of either 30 or 35 seconds in high school games.) These physical and time pressures can wreak havoc with one's shooting accuracy. Only the free throw, as its name suggests, is spared such potential interference (although a player officially has only ten seconds to take such a shot).

What secondary targets exist in the game of basketball? Well, player roles overlap, but typically positions and duties line up as follows:

1) Point guard: On offense, he strives to dribble the ball down the court with an eye toward passing it to another player either close to the basket or wide open for an outside shot. A good point guard is adept at bounce passes, skip passes (in the air across the court), and alley-oop passes (lobs near the rim of the basket that may be caught and slam dunked by a teammate). Taking a long shot or penetrating toward the basket for a shorter one is certainly an option. Defensively, the point guard targets the ball, trying to knock it loose from an opposing ball handler, intercept a pass, deflect a

shot or pass, etc. The point guard has primary responsibility for receiving outlet passes from rebounding teammates, leading fast breaks, signaling set plays and defenses to his team, and serving as the "quarterback" on the court.

2) Shooting guard: As befits her title, the #2 guard works to be a dead-eye outside shooter from several different locations on the floor, hopefully some of them three-point shots. But she also has secondary responsibility for ball-handling and passing the ball within the flow of the offense. She penetrates to the hoop when an opening shows itself, and gets back down the court quickly during defensive transitions and fast break opportunities.

3) Small forward: The shooting forward likes to have medium-range and three-point jump shots within his skill set, along with slashing moves to the basket and the prowess needed for offensive put-backs. He must be ready to rebound, offensively or defensively, with an eye toward passing or shooting as the situation warrants. Not only is the basket a target, of course; one focuses on the ball on defense with an eye toward stealing it. Even one's opposing player may be considered a target for one's attention, particularly in a man-to-man defense. Playing zone defense, one's target is a region to cover and any opposing player who may venture into it.

4) Power forward: Usually the second tallest, strongest, heaviest player on a squad, the PF needs an inside game: a repertoire of post moves, short shots, and rebounding skills. She must have a strong will and fearless approach to banging into opposing players in this supposedly non-contact sport. Teammates and coaches appreciate leaping

and shot-blocking skills, as well. An interior player, the power forward needs to be able to pass out to an open shooter or down-court to a teammate in transition. Again, the basket is the most valuable, stationary target, but moving targets abound in basketball, too.

5) Center: Normally the tallest player on a team plays the post position, weaving in and out of the key near the basket on offense in anticipation of a pass for a short shot or dunk. He would do well to be able to flash out to the high post, as well, in order to take a medium-range jump shot or pass to a teammate cutting to the basket. The center tries to use his height, wingspan, and bulk to thwart adversaries' attempts at lay-ups and alley-oop passes, block out for rebounds, and pass over the outstretched arms of shorter players. When his team employs a full-court press, it is usually the center that runs down court to stand near the basket as the last line of defense should the opposition break the press and attack on the run.

The aforementioned roles, as mentioned, may blur, and the positions themselves are far from set in stone; when occasions warranted, Magic Johnson spent time playing all five positions for the Los Angeles Lakers. Going for the ball defensively, or shooting to score offensively, may sometimes be best accomplished by playing four relatively short and quick players (guards) and only one big man (center or forward). Some teams lack a stereotypical center and opt for three forwards. Variations on the theme give opposing players and coaches more to think about and defend against.

The constant, flowing interaction among basketball players resembles the mass of runners and traders that fill the floor of the New York Stock Exchange---alert, vigilant, quick-thinking, and actively decisive. Individuals swirl among friends and foes following orders and set plays, making split-second alterations, improvising as circumstances warrant, and flowing from target to target. A jazz ensemble, though typically stationary, resembles a basketball team in that its members blend together collectively and improvise individually. If team chemistry is right, a team of basketball players can make beautiful "music" together.

There is one element of basketball that should, in theory, be characterized by a high degree of accuracy: the free throw. Game action stops. Time pressures subside (except for the seldom-enforced ten-second limit to shoot). The shooter stands at a line 15 feet from the basket, facing the hoop straight on. The benefits of practice are strong. During one day of his team's after-practice routines in 1975, Canton, NY high school player, Hal Cohen, sank 598 consecutive free throws. That proves that a repetitive motion can be grooved to hit the target with powerful consistency. But why didn't Hal repeat his fete while playing in college, for Syracuse University? Game conditions can be quite disruptive to the foul shooting process. The player may arrive at the free throw line short of breath, with heart pounding, due to the exertions of the game. The pressure to make the shot, to help one's team win, can be intense. Spectators may test the boundaries of good sportsmanship by yelling, making noises, booing, waving their arms behind the basket in perceptually distorting ways, etc. I once saw Syracuse students raise a life-size photograph of a bikini-clad beauty directly behind the basket just as a player was about to launch his shots; he missed both. A Duke student who stood and danced wearing nothing but a skimpy Speedo swimsuit had the same effect (and became a YouTube sensation). Even opposing players can get in on the act, stepping up behind a shooter to whisper some snide remark, or trading places with one another across the lane just before the player gets the ball to take aim.

So, how accurate have the best players been at this clearly targeted aspect of the sport of basketball? The record for most consecutive free throws ever made in game situations was set by none other than the legendary John Wooden during the span 1934-36; he made 138 in a row. Close behind was female record-holder, Deb Remmerde, an NAIA player, who canned 133 free throws in succession in 2005-6. The modern NCAA men's record is held by Darnell Archey of Butler from 2000-2003, during which he made 85 straight. The women's NCAA Division I record is in the hands of Ginny Doyle who made 66 straight for Richmond during 1990-92. In the National Basketball Association (NBA), the record was 97 by Michael Williams in 1993. In the Women's NBA, Eva Nemcova made 66 in a row during the 1999-2000 season. Percentage-wise, Eva set the one-season standard of 98.4%; Stacy Frese holds the WNBA career mark of 91.7%. Adrienne Squire of Penn State made 96.4 % of her free throws during her collegiate career; Blake Ahearn of Missouri State set the men's standard by sinking 94.6% of his shots at the charity stripe. In the NBA, the career honor goes to Mark Price (90.39%) while Calvin Murphy holds the one-year standard of 95.8%.

Most basketball fans know that Wilt Chamberlain once scored 100 points in a professional game (in 1962). He holds the NBA single-season record for field goal percentage at 72.7%; another giant, Artis Gilmore, made 59.9% of his shots from the field across his lengthy NBA career. Most would not be surprised to know that Michael Jordan scored 10 or more points in a game 866 times between 1986 and 2001. The ball, half the diameter of its target, <u>can</u> be put through the basket. But don't let sparkling statistics such as these mislead you into believing that basketball is a relatively easy game. It offers a kaleidoscope of target-oriented action. Players run and jump, pass and shoot, block and steal, in dynamic team interaction. The sport demands an awesome blend of athleticism, fitness, and mental agility to succeed in battling opponents and hitting the targets—whether baskets or teammates—a high percentage of the time.

Football

In terms of the variety of targets and complexity of roles of various player positions, football resembles baseball. The overriding goal, of course, is to move the ball into any portion of the end zone for a six-point touchdown. In that event, two additional points may be earned by running or passing the ball into that 10 by 53 1/3-yard-wide area. Alternately, a team may opt to attempt to kick the ball through the 18 1/2-foot-wide uprights for an extra point after a touchdown. Short of scoring a touchdown, a specialized player may kick the ball through the goal posts (above the upright) to claim a three-point field goal for his team. But, as I say, the game is far from straightforward and bears rich analysis.

Football is organized mayhem. Players are assigned distinct roles according to position. Plays are devised, drawn up, learned, and practiced by offense and defense alike. The teams take the field ready to execute their game plans. Then all heck breaks loose!

When the ball is snapped, violent collisions send players every which way. Receivers get bumped off course at the line of scrimmage—or break into the open without a defender in sight. The quarterback drops back to pass, safe within the pocket created by his trusty offensive linemen, only to be sacked by an unseen, fast-running cornerback blitzing from the blind side. A running back takes a handoff and streaks for the gap in the line and open field beyond, only to slip on the turf, bump into a teammate, or get hammered by a linebacker who has shed his blocker. The wind blows passes and kicks off-course. Receivers drop balls that hit them in the hands or on their numbers—or stretch out to make incredible one-handed grabs.

At the center of the storm, carrying the primary burden of responsibility for the offense, is the quarterback (QB). He must keep multiple targets in mind at once. The end zone looms large in his thinking, but he typically tries to advance toward that ultimate target by degrees. His first target on any play is the ball, hiked to him by the center from a proximate location or several paces removed—i.e., in shotgun or pistol formation. Once that transaction is safely conducted, the QB has another reasonably tried-and-true option which is to hand off to a running back; the QB aims for the runner's midsection while the runner must watch the ball into his grasp—or else risk a fumble—while almost simultaneously looking ahead to where it's best to run—or else risk getting dropped for a loss in the backfield. If the QB opts to pass, of course, he almost always aims for a moving target: a wide receiver, tight end, fullback, or tailback. Forward passes are most readily accomplished by the quarterback who has a special sense: an ability to visualize the juncture where he can toss the spinning pigskin to arrive exactly where a would-be receiver will arrive while running. It's easier said than done. That's because eleven defensive players share the objective of thwarting the effort. Their assorted targets include the eligible receivers (bumping them, staying close to them), the QB's eyes (which can be "read" to forecast the path of his pass), the QB himself (for the esteemed sack), and the ball (up in the air for an interception).

Before the ball is even hiked, the QB needs to focus on plays signaled or called from the sideline, the defensive alignment before him—in case he best "check" the play and change to something more likely to succeed—and the positions of his teammates, including those who may shift or go into motion before the actual snap of the ball. It's nerve-wracking, complicated business. The best quarterbacks are confident and effective multi-taskers—again, doing a series of actions in rapid sequence rather than all at once.

Here's how the position was described by John Brodie, former All-Pro Quarterback of the San Francisco 49ers:

> A quarterback is a kind of juggler. The trick is to keep a whole lot of Indian clubs up in the air—or floating in your mind—and the more experience you have, the more

Indian clubs you can juggle…breaking the huddle, getting the numbers barked out right—and you've got the playbook in your head, hoping you can call the right one at the right time…And this means learning to juggle all the other details you have continually to take into account: the score, the quarter, the down, yards to go, time remaining, the number of time outs, the weather, the wind, the conditions of the field, the conditions of your men—who's high, who's low, who's hurt—and also the condition of the men on the other team—who's strong, who's not so strong, who's slowing down (Brodie & Houston, 1974, pp. 183-4).

Running the offense of a football team is a complicated target game.

As for those who literally run the football, after receiving a pass or a hand-off, running backs have their target clearly in mind: the end zone for a touchdown. They'll settle for a nice gain, or even just falling forward or flashing enough forward progress to gain a first down. After all, large, strong, fast opposing players are targeting their legs and torsos to tackle them before they can gain ground. Defenders may specifically target the ball, striving to knock or rip it out of the possession of the ball carrier—a fumble that goes up for grabs by any member of either team. Runners need the agility to evade tacklers and the guts to collide with them en route to forward progress toward the team's goal.

What other target shooters man a football team? The placekicker typically uses a sidewinding action to boot the ball through the uprights, over the goal post. Immediately following a touchdown, with the ball being hiked from the three-yard line in college football, it's a high-probability task worth one point. The center, often a specialist known as the long snapper, must first direct the ball crisply to the holder, another specialist who's kneeling sideways to catch and hurriedly place the ball just right so the kicker can make solid contact with it. Any inaccuracy in that preliminary process can lead to an off-target kick. Meanwhile, of course, the snap of the ball by the center triggers a stampede of beefy guys. Eleven opposing players are targeting the ball—rushing around the end, lunging outward, or leaping upward at the line of scrimmage to knock the ball off-course, disrupt the timing of the play, or at least distract the kicker. When a longer kick is needed, as for a field goal or the recently elongated extra point in the NFL, the kicker may need to launch the ball at a lower trajectory; this increases the chance the defense can block it.

The kicker also, naturally, kicks off. He aims to strike the ball squarely so as to knock it high, long, and straight—hopefully into the far end zone but, alternately, away from the opposing team's best kick returner. The punter, similarly, aims to strike the ball solidly in a certain direction, hoping to pin the opposing team inside its 20-yard line. Then the kicker or the punter becomes a hunter, aiming to tackle the kick/punt returner should he evade tackling by the rest of the kicking team.

It should be noted that America's neighbor to the north, Canada, plays the game of football with some modifications. The Canadian Football League (CFL) plays on a larger field: 110 vs

100 yards long, 65 vs. 53 1/3 yards wide, with end zones that are 20 vs. 10 yards deep. There is more room to move with a larger target in mind. Teams have 12 instead of 11 players on a side, though both the NFL and CFL require 7 players on the line of scrimmage. The two offensive ends in Canada have the option of moving along the line before the snap of the ball, if they wish. Not only that, but the entire offensive backfield, with the exception of the QB, may be in motion before the snap. Hence, would-be pass receivers may have running starts across the line of scrimmage at the moment the ball is hiked. Given only 3 downs, instead of 4, to gain 10 yards before having to surrender the ball to the opposing team, CFL play may seem more challenging in that one respect. But since the defenders must line up one full yard (vs. 11 inches) from the line of scrimmage, many teams gamble on third-and-one situations. Clock stoppages occur after every play beyond the three-minute warning near the end of each half; late-game comebacks are so common that the CFL has adopted a motto of "No Lead Is Safe". There are more differences, too numerous to mention, between NFL and CFL rules. Canadian is an interesting variant of American football!

Moving targets, pigskin and human, are the nature of the game of football. It's little wonder that youngsters participate in punt, pass, and kick competitions to prove their prowess performing all three critical elements of football as a target game. Then the biggest, fastest, strongest, and most highly skilled move into the game of football itself—opening their bodies and minds to the risks of concussions, knee damage, shoulder injuries, and assorted other health hazards.

Golf

Ah, here's an individual sport without all of the complications endemic to most team sports. Even in team competitions, such as the Ryder Cup, President's Cup, or Solheim Cup, only the individual player taking the shot is responsible for its outcome. And it seems an unambiguous target game: One tees off from a designated rectangle of closely cropped grass, launching the ball from between two tee markers (and as far as ten feet behind them) and aiming to put (usually putt) the dimpled ball into the four-inch diameter cup a couple-few hundred yards away. Several factors aid the process: (1) the ball is stationary; (2) so is the target; (3) the golfer may stare at the target of her swing for as long as desired; (4) golfers carry 14 clubs from which to choose, tailoring the tool to the task; (5) playing partners and spectators are hushed into silence in order to enable the player to concentrate. It must be a relatively easy game, right?

Well, of course, there is just a little more to the game than that. For one thing, the golfer must look away from the secondary target—the fairway, green, or hole toward which she hopes to direct the ball. That goal must be fixed solely in the mind's eye. The golf ball, with a diameter of 1.68 inches, is a rather small primary target to be struck with a clubhead moving at speeds over 100 mph. Unlike a baseball, that may be hit as far as 400 or 500 feet, the golf ball is being sent on a journey of 200, 300, or more yards. There is small margin for error; even a slight side spin imparted to the ball at impact can send it careening far off course into woods, water, or sand. Wind and weather can wreak havoc with any shot. The goal of the game, of course, is to cover several hundred yards with as few shots as possible before knocking the little white sphere into a cup just over twice its diameter. Just as baseball batters sometimes lose their balance swinging at their moving targets, so do golfers sometimes sway too much to strike their immobile targets with the proper blend of force and precision required. A golf swing looks downright unnatural. The lengthy club is brought to and fro in a diagonal arc that requires a stable yet fluid stance. Even the slightest deviation in balance can result in a hit distorted enough to send the ball off course (sometimes literally out of bounds). Wrists must cock and release with exquisite timing in order to impart force and direction to the hard-covered little ball. A golfer must strive to begin, and remain, as centered as possible in order to achieve a hit in the "sweet spot" of the clubface.

Different circumstances require various shots. Golf is decidedly a thinking person's game. Should I try to hit over, under, or around that tree limb that obstructs my path toward the green? In what direction is the wind blowing, at what velocity, and with what probable impact on the flight of my golf ball? How can I best adjust? With the pin only a few paces from the front of the green, or near a water hazard, where should I aim to maximize my chance not only to land my shot on the green but also to stop it within reasonable putting distance of the hole? An uphill stance…a downhill one…a sidehill lie…a ball in deep rough…a tree branch limiting the backswing…a ball partially buried in the sand…a ball in a divot…a twig resting against the ball—all require adjustments to strike the ball with authority and accuracy. Match vs. stroke play—trying merely to win a hole by any margin in order to defeat an individual or pair of opponents, vs. accountability for each and every swing or stroke in order to score better than an entire tournament field—further complicates thinking and strategy.

As with baseball, basketball, football, et al., there can be enormous pressure to perform, some of it externally imposed by fans or prize money, but more commonly internally generated—nothing challenges one's self-esteem and frustration tolerance more than the game of golf. The stress and payoff of golf mount as one nears the target—chipping and putting.

Hitting a drive or long shot requires muscular exertion which, in turn, needs a fairly high level of physiological arousal for its execution. As a golfer approaches or reaches the green, however, she must tone down that level of activation. The short game requires stillness and sense of touch. Distance control is valuable throughout the sport, but the demand for precision increases for the shorter strokes. The same goes for visualization. It's valuable to be able to imagine a long shot—see it in one's mind's eye, anticipate the feeling of it—arc toward the fairway or green. It's essential to be able to read the subtle contours of a green, feel little undulations under one's feet, foresee the path on which the ball will roll, and judge the pace at which the ball must travel to finish near, or in, the hole. Golfers need steady nerves and attentional control.

HOCKEY

Like golfers, hockey players also wield sticks and swing at a primary target in the hope of guiding it into a secondary target. Of course, they have only one stick, not 14, use relatively truncated swings, and must hit a rapidly moving target. The puck is nearly always on the go. Players aim to hit that puck at a goal (6 feet wide by 4 feet high) similar in size to that of lacrosse. They have teammates to help them by passing them the puck in locations and times that are conducive to goal-scoring. But that 6-ounce vulcanized rubber puck, moving up to 100 mph, sure hurts if it hits you. So do the body checks, stick checks, and occasional punches that are designed to divert the player from his/her goal. Add to that the speed with which this game is played, skating on a slippery surface that works against the rapid changes of direction players need, and it's no wonder that few goals are typically scored in hockey games. Baseball hitters and golfers stand still, centered, to swing at the ball; hockey players do everything on the fly.

As with other major team sports, there are important differences among the various positions on the ice. Forwards carry the bulk of responsibility for shots on goal. Defensemen do as their name suggests, interfere with the progress of opposing players in the hope of stealing, or at least deflecting, shots and passes. The center occupies the space on the ice that her title implies, though with a great deal of latitude regarding where to move according to the flow of the game.

The goaltender naturally has a primary goal on which to focus: the puck. She must track wherever it travels, shifting position as needed to guard against shots and deflections from myriad angles. The goalie's goal is to catch, block, deflect, trap, or otherwise stop it from passing through the crease and crossing the goal line toward or into the net. It can be exceedingly hard to keep track of the fast-moving puck. Opposing players, or even teammates, might block the vision of the goalie, disabling her ability to see a shot coming. One can be in perfect position to block a shot, only to leave a wide-open shot by a player on the other side of the goal who receives an on-target pass. Some shots deflect off the sticks or skates of players, one's teammate or the other team's player. The goalie has other goals besides stopping shots. She may venture from the net to steer an off-target shot to a teammate. She strives to be aware of other players who stray close, bracing herself to direct her defense against that player should she receive a pass from an opposing teammate.

Hockey also, of course, includes set plays and strategies conceived by its coaches and practiced by the team in order to maximize the chance of scoring. Defensive schemes, naturally, strive to thwart the opposing team. Power play situations, given that one team or other has a man-up advantage via penalty, demand special consideration. Hockey may be a relatively low-scoring game, but its aggressive, skillful, and fast-flowing nature make it highly challenging to play and exciting to watch.

Soccer

All you need are some open space, a ball, and some sort of goal toward which to kick that ball. Given the simplicity of those requirements, access to this sport is nearly universal. Most people world-wide, regardless of socio-economic status and life circumstances, can play the game. Its low-cost availability is one reason that football is the planet's most popular sport.

In addition, soccer may be relatively unchallenging. After all, the official goal is large (24 feet wide and 8 feet high, for international play) and the ball is a nice, highly visible, manageable size. Nobody tries to thwart you using sticks (think hockey and lacrosse). As in basketball, bodily contact that is purportedly against the rules is punished, usually, by officials patrolling the contest. You have lots of teammates to help you toward the goal. Of course, there are also the same number of opposing players trying to thwart you, and those players still manage to get in some licks and kicks away from the eyes of officials. Competition to possess the ball is intense and must be accomplished primarily with the feet. The ball may seem small relative to its expansive goal, but agile goalies and their fellow defenders can do a lot to block access to it. Adept foot-play, pinpoint passing, curved shot-making, and impeccable timing are usually required to hit one's target. That could explain the plethora of 1-0 scores in this sport.

All soccer players on the grass or artificial playing surface—forwards, midfielders, defensemen—have the ball as the primary target and the goal as the secondary one. There are intermediate goals, of course—i.e., passes to teammates. The rules of soccer, or football as it is called in most countries other than the United States (where football is an entirely different sport), require that players contact and advance the ball using only their legs and feet. Soccer is a head game, as well, since one's noggin is another legitimate tool for striking the ball. With all the concern about concussions in American football, you must wonder about the dangers of head shots in international football. Apparently, such injuries are uncommon. Soccer is far from a safe, injury-free sport, however.

Among the most common injuries are ankle sprains, muscle pulls and tears, damaged joints, and bodily bruises.

Soccer combines team strategy, individual execution, and free-wheeling adaptation to circumstances. Team loyalties and rivalries are intense; just observe rabid fan reactions. Players need massive amounts of stamina, agile eye-foot coordination, and "vision" of where to kick the ball given the flow of teammates and opposing players on the large field of play. Thus, international football packs a great deal of complexity into its simplistic framework. No wonder the sport of soccer commands the most popularity world-wide.

Tennis

A tennis ball is a fast-moving, spinning, bouncing target that demands visual tracking ability in order to hit it solidly. Similar to baseball and golf, the player cannot directly see the secondary target—the opponent's court—at the moment of impact, but nevertheless must try to place each shot in exacting locations. Unlike a baseball player or golfer, who stands in one place while swinging at the ball, the tennis player usually needs the agility to do so on the run. Serves approach at blinding speeds; Americans Roscoe Tanner (153 mph), Andy Roddick (155), and John Isner (157) have blasted balls that are difficult to return, and Australian Samuel Groth once hit a 163.7 mph court burner. Even with the seeming advantage of a big flat implement with which to strike the ball, it is no simple task to serve, volley, and rally with consistent effectiveness.

Tennis does not demand that a player aim for a specific target, only an area that is 27 by 39 feet for singles play, and 36 by 39 for doubles; games begin with serves that must land within a rectangle measuring 13.5 by 21 feet, a challenging target that begins just over the net. The net, by the way, stands officially 3' 6" at the posts and 3' high in the center. A point is scored if one manages not only to strike the ball into that designated region, but that one's opponent does not return it to the in-bounds area on the other side of the net. Forehand slams, one- and two-handed backhands, topspin lobs, cut shots, drop shots, overhead slams, and various curving shots make it interesting!

World-class tennis players appear to epitomize physical fitness. Nearly every muscle in the body must be well-developed to enable a player to move with cat-like reflexes, run at high speeds, change direction on a dime, and hammer the ball with the velocity needed to get it past a comparably fit opponent. Variations in playing surfaces complicate matters by altering the bounce, spin, and speed of tennis balls striking them; grass (Wimbleton) is the fastest surface and clay (French Open) the slowest, with hard-court surfaces (e.g., Deco Turf in the U.S. Open and Plexicushion in the Australian Open) somewhere in between. It's common for a player's dominant arm to be larger than her other one, because of the demands of serving and hitting with that primary hand. But any such asymmetry must not cause muscle strain or injury or the match is lost. Endurance is key. In pro tournaments, women typically play the best of three sets, and men the best of five; the latter, in particular, can last as long as several hours if the match is tight and the outcome requires numerous deuce games, tie-breakers, and/or additional games in order to win a final set by a margin of two games.

Tennis matches are contested around the world, in all sorts of climates. It's a fair-weather sport—rain (or snow!) makes the playing surface too slippery for traction and safety. Hot weather, of course, can tax one's endurance. The whimsies of wind and sunlight can interfere with a player's vision and execution, but those factors usually even out since players routinely switch sides of the court. Audiences can add to the pressure to win, though codes of conduct prohibit spectators from distracting players from the focus they need to play their high-speed, high-stakes sport effectively.

CHAPTER 3

Mid-Major Sports

• • •

THESE SPORTS HAVE LOWER LEVELS of notoriety than do the aforementioned endeavors, yet they have broad appeal among both participants and spectators.

Bowling
Cricket
Field Hockey
Lacrosse
Softball

BOWLING

Bowling looks easy. Played in ideal indoor conditions, the goal is to knock down only ten pins with a ball that is large and dense relative to them. Those pins stand in a uniform formation only 60 feet from where the bowler releases the shot. If it's not easy enough to bowl over those pins the first time, you get an extra shot to finish the job. The combination of eye-hand coordination (you may focus on the pins themselves or on other markers en route to guide your aim) and practice should make high scoring a breeze.

Of course, the "strike zone" has a rather small margin for error, the ball tends to spin and glide in variable fashion, and the weight of the ball can tax one's balance. Is it any wonder that bowlers complain of even more back problems than the #2 source of referrals for back treatment, golf? The ten pins may be neatly set in their triangular pattern, ready to fall down in domino-like fashion, but the impact between their cylindrical shapes and the spherical ball make for some unpredictable scattering of such targets. If your first shot misses the "pocket", those pesky "splits" can be challenging to convert into spares! Above all, keep your mind out of the gutter.

CRICKET

How does this sport merit consideration in this list of widespread, challenging sports? Well, to begin with, it's the world's second-most popular sport! Only soccer attracts more participants and fans. Cricket is rather overlooked on the American athletic landscape, but the sport occupies major interest in the United Kingdom and most former members of the British Commonwealth (e.g., India, Pakistan, Australia, the West Indies). Secondly, cricket is a team game with numerous complicated rules of play, and it's a sport requiring broad athletic skills.

Cricket is a bat-and-ball game contested on a large field ("ground") by two teams of eleven players apiece. Two umpires uphold the many rules on the ground, with a third umpire available to oversee decisions with the aid of slow-motion video replays. Teams bat in successive innings and try to score the most runs, but that may be the extent of the sport's similarity to baseball. Let's examine some specifics.

The cricket ground is a roughly elliptical, flat field of grass ranging in length from 90 to 150 meters (100-160 yards) across. In the center of the ground is the rectangular "pitch", a strip that extends between two "wickets" (each of which consists of three vertical stumps/sticks of wood stuck into the grass). Each batsman wields a willow bat that is flat on one side and humped on the other; the blade has a maximum length of 38 inches and maximum width of 4.25 inches. The ball resembles a baseball in size, hardness, and leather covering; its circumference is 8.8 to 9.0 inches and it weighs between 5.5 and 5.75 ounces. But the ball's leather covering is thick and hemispheric. It's usually red with white stitching, though white balls may be used in night games for greater visibility.

In baseball, the pitcher usually begins moving with a wind-up motion (at the rubber on the mound) leading toward his delivery of the ball; in cricket, the pitcher (bowler) gets a running start from well outside the pitch area. He then hurls the ball toward his target, the wooden wicket. A batsman defends his wicket, swinging to strike the ball into (or beyond) the field of play. On contact, the batsman begins to run toward the opposite wicket while his comrade batsman at the other end of the pitch runs in contrary direction; that is, the batsmen run to each other's end of the pitch. Meanwhile fielders strive to throw the ball toward the target, the wicket, to get the runner out or at least stop more runs from being scored. If the ball eludes the bare-handed fielders and stays in play, the batsmen may run back and forth multiple times, with each successful transit scoring a run. If the batsman hits the ball past the boundary of the field, after the ball hits the ground (and bounces or rolls), 4 runs are scored; if the ball soars past the boundary without first striking the ground (like a baseball home run), 6 runs are awarded. If the bowler gets the ball past the batsman and hits his wicket, it's an out. If a fielder catches a hit ball in the air, before it hits the ground, it's an out. There are at least eight other ways that outs can be recorded. Yet outs can be hard to come by.

A "test cricket" match, the most common type of game, consists of only two innings of ten outs each. But matches can endure for a maximum of five days! They must be high-scoring affairs.

Cricket, then, is a sport with multiple targets. Players in long-running competitions need speed, agility, eye-hand coordination, freedom from distractibility, and a good measure of endurance. Given all of its rules and complications, it must be challenging to learn how to play. Fans must be knowledgeable and patient, as well!

FIELD HOCKEY

As its name reveals, this sport is hockey off-ice. As such, it's a much slower-moving sport than that played by ice skaters. But it surely has its elements of difficulty. Played with a hard, spherical ball rather than a puck, with that ball's being navigated by sticks that are shorter than those used on the rink, field hockey requires strategy, teamwork, and athleticism galore. And that posture that players must maintain to reach down to the ball with those shorter sticks (31-38 inches or 80-95 centimeters long) must risk wear-and-tear on one's spine and musculature. Players all use "right-handed" sticks, flat on their left-side bottom curved portions, and rounded on their right sides, and may touch the ball only with those flat surfaces; if a back-handed shot is desired, the player may rotate the stick 180 degrees and use the flat that way. Only the goalie (protecting the goal 12 feet wide by 7 feet high) is permitted to contact the ball with any part of her stick or body.

Contact happens in this relatively non-contact sport. Competitors are allowed to tackle their opponents from the front or side while attempting to take away the ball. Officials call fouls and penalties, for tackles from behind or balls lifted into the air too close to players' heads, for instance, and getting hit with the stick (traditionally wood but more likely fiberglass, kevlar, or carbon-fiber composite in the modern era) can hurt. The ball is usually hard plastic over cork, typically white, with dimpled indentations to reduce aquaplaning on wet playing fields. Games may be played rain or shine. Those fields ("pitches") used to be all grass, but artificial surfaces 60 yards wide by 100 yards long now outnumber natural fields.

In the U.S., field hockey is usually associated with women's collegiate teams. World-wide competitions have been dominated the past few decades by teams from the Netherlands, Australia, and Argentina. But men also compete around the globe; Pakistan used to dominate, but pre-eminent men's teams since the 1980's have included Netherlands, Germany, New Zealand, Australia, and Spain.

Do field hockey players get to wear protective clothing? Only the goalie may, covered with headgear, leg guards, kickers, and gloves. When field players are called upon to defend against a penalty shot, they may don face masks for that occasion. The ten players from each team on the pitch at any time typically play designated roles of defender (3), midfielder (4), or forward (3). Passing, stealing, shooting, tackling, and running team plays on the fly make field hockey a difficult, hazardous, and rewarding sport.

Lacrosse

Compared to field hockey, collegiate lacrosse players aim for a somewhat smaller goal (6-feet square) with a smaller ball (about 2.5 inches in diameter). They also play in all kinds of weather, but that does not affect the course of the dense ball they propel through the air with baskets on the ends of sticks. Of course, opposing players are using their sticks for another purpose—to block your shot, whack your body, or otherwise get the ball for their own target practice. And the game is played in motion, with fatigue and hazards aplenty. That's why lacrosse claims to be "the fastest game on two feet". Given the density of the hard rubber ball, and the velocity with which it can be whipped with a lacrosse stick, there is just cause for players to wear protective padding and helmets with face masks.

Rules vary considerably among pro, college, high school, and youth versions of lacrosse, as well as between the men's and women's games. Field lacrosse is played at high levels by elite college teams on grass or artificial fields measuring 110 by 60 yards (100 by 55 meters); the goal lies within a circular crease that is 18 feet in diameter. Box lacrosse is played in smaller arenas, so the goal is only 4 x 4 feet; since it is contested in professional leagues, it's a rougher sport that permits more physical cross-checking by players. On the other end of the spectrum, women's lacrosse discourages aggressive physicality; female players may wear only face masks (goggles) and mouth guards, with thin gloves sometimes, too. Men typically wear protective gloves, arm pads, shoulder pads, and full-face helmets; box lacrosse players add rib pads to protect themselves from the pain of cross-checking. Goalies, naturally, may wear more protective gear.

What makes lacrosse a challenging sport besides the running, team play (ten on a side including the goalie), passing, shooting, strategizing, and substituting on the fly? That little ball weighs 140-147 grams (4.9-5.2 ounces) and can pack a wallop when propelled by sticks that vary in length from 40 (short, for attackmen) to 72 (long, for defensemen) inches in length. The shafts of those sticks may be composed of aluminum alloy, titanium, scandium, composite, or wood; within certain guidelines, lacrosse sticks may be wielded to whack opponents to slow, stop, or steal from them. Jim Brown is considered by many to have been the greatest, most punishing running back in pro football history, but observers of his exploits at Syracuse University contend that the big, fast bruiser was even more imposing and successful on the lacrosse field. Given the toughness, agility, speed, endurance, eye-hand coordination, and teamwork needed to play this game, it is no surprise that it is growing in popularity across the U.S. Professional leagues have emerged.

Softball

Yes, this is simply baseball with a larger ball to hit, throw, and catch. Its being softer, of course, might make it easier to handle---there's less sting when it hits one's glove. And the pitching is underhand rather than overhand, so the speed of the game must necessarily be more civilized. But the dimensions of the playing field are comparable to those of baseball. As in baseball, it can be highly challenging to hit the ball over the fence or into the outfield where an opposing player cannot catch it on the fly. Each position has its respective responsibilities. The pitcher and catcher, as in baseball, must multi-task in mind-boggling fashion. Underhand softball pitches do not attain the velocity of overhand baseball pitches, but their speeds of 75 mph for women and 85 mph for men are hot to handle. One can still get struck with the ball and, even if it's softer and slightly slower-moving, it still hurts plenty.

CHAPTER 4

Summer Olympic Sports

• • •

EVERY FOUR YEARS, AFTER INTENSE periods of training and tryouts to qualify for their national teams, the world's best athletes congregate to vie for gold, silver, and bronze medals in these (and other) audience-appealing sports:

Archery
Athletics (Track & Field)
Badminton
Basketball
Boxing
Canoe Slalom (& Sprint)
Cycling (BMX, Mountain Bike, Road, & Track)
Decathlon
Diving
Equestrian (Dressage, Eventing, & Jumping)
Gymnastics (Artistic & Rhythmic)
Handball
Heptathlon
Judo
Modern Pentathlon

Rhythmic Gymnastics
Rowing
Rugby
Sailing
Shooting
Swimming
Synchronized Swimming
Table Tennis
Taekwondo
Tennis
Trampolining
Triathlon
Volleyball (Team & Beach)
Water Polo
Weightlifting
Wrestling (Freestyle & Greco-Roman)

Archery

This quintessential target sport is contested at the Olympic level every four years. Archers use recurve bows to take aim on a bull's eye centered on the target of concentric circles 70 meters away. During the ranking round, 64 archers shoot 6 x 12 arrows apiece. After their scores are ranked and converted into seedings, a match play system eliminates competitors until only two remain to shoot for the gold and silver medals. Since 1984, Korean men have won team gold 4 of 7 Olympic competitions. Even more impressive, perhaps, have been the Korean women; during the same time span, they have won 14 of 15 individual gold medals.

Athletics (Track & Field)

Here's an assortment of sports that obviously combine speed, power, and distance as competitors run, walk, jump, and/or throw. Analysis reveals that each event has some target-oriented aspects.

Discus

The objective, of course, is to hurl a metal disc as far as one can. That is not a fully straightforward proposition because of the parameters involved. The contestant begins on a circular pad 8.25 feet (2.5 meters) in diameter within which he or she revs up—literally spinning the body to build up speed and momentum—before releasing the disc into a target area that opens up progressively (into a 34.92-degree sector) before him or her. That landing zone seems wide, but there is little margin for error; during the high-speed exertion of the throw, even small mistakes make off-target tosses that go shorter distances or fly out of bounds completely. Adding to the complexity, of course, is the disc itself. Men toss a lenticular (biconvex, shaped like a lentil) disc weighing 2 kilograms (4.4 pounds) with a diameter of 8.5 inches (.219 meters); junior men (aged 18-19) throw a slightly lighter disc (1.75 kilograms) and youth boys a still lighter one (1.5 kilograms). Women competitors of all ages launch a 1-kilogram (2.2-pound) disc that is 7 inches (.18 meters) in diameter. The difficulty of mastering the spinning throwing technique—requiring strength, speed, and balance galore—needs experience; most top discus competitors achieve their best tosses (over 70 meters) at age 30 or beyond.

Hammer Throw

An ancient weapon is converted into an athletic competition as participants heave a dense sphere, resembling a cannon ball, attached to a steel wire to enable added distance. The men throw a steel ball that weighs 16 pounds (7.257 kilograms), while the women compete with a sphere that weighs 8.82 pounds (4 kilograms). The total length of the apparatus, from handle through wire through ball, is 3' 11 3/4" (121.5 centimeters) for the men and 3' 11" (119.5 centimeters) for the women. To hurl such a contraption into a 35-degree sector while staying within a 7-foot diameter throwing circle requires a deft blend of strength, balance, and technique. After about two swings of the hammer in stationary position, the thrower rotates 3 or 4 (or sometimes 5) times using complicated heel-toe foot movements before unleashing the hammer into the air. Woe to the competitor who is susceptible to motion sickness! Yurly Sedykh's 1986 world record heave of 86.74 meters (284' 6 3/4") still stands; the women's mark of 81.08 meters (266 feet) was set recently, in 2015, by Anita Wlodarczyk.

High Jump

Do high jumpers take aim on a target? They sure do—a lofty one. A high jumper aims not to hit an object, move a ball into a goal, or do anything requiring pinpoint accuracy—except, of course, clearing a crossbar that stands above his/her own height. A high jumper has interim goals in her approach to the ultimate objective. Her footwork, pacing, angular lean, and bodily movements must be precisely choreographed and executed flawlessly to ensure a lift-off at just the right moment, the optimal distance from the bar, with her muscles gathered for maximal spring and perfect form. Most competitors use an approach of 8 to 13 strides, with build-up of speed to generate forward and upward momentum. Elite leapers employ the famous "Fosbury Flop", launching themselves head first with their backs to the bar. Using this style, jumpers Franklin Jacobs and Stefan Holm managed to ascend nearly two feet over their own personal heights. Male and female world records held by Javier Sotomayor (2.45 meters = 8' 1/4") and Stefka Kostadinova (2.09 meters = 6' 10 1/4 ") were set in 1993 and 1987, respectively; more recent jumpers have come close but been unable to surpass those long-standing marks.

JAVELIN

Now here's a field event that seems more obviously target-oriented. At least the practitioner is hurling an object toward an objective. The goal is maximal distance. That achievement depends upon the athleticism, musculature, and timing of the javelin thrower. A great heave is accomplished not only by gaining forward speed and using proper form, but also by launching the javelin at exactly the right angle of elevation. Eye-body coordination helps achieve that end, one complication being that the thrower must be aware of the boundary line on the ground while focusing on the angle of launch into the sky. Taking into account wind conditions, sunlight or rain, one's standing vis-à-vis fellow competitors, etc., complicates matters. Men carefully yet swiftly move down a runway that is 4 meters (13 feet) wide and 30 meters (98 feet) long to fling a fiberglass spear weighing 800 grams (28 ounces) that is 2.6 - 2.7 meters (8' 6" - 8' 10") in length. Women throw a slightly smaller javelin, 2.2 - 2.3 meters (7' 3" - 7' 7") in length with a weight of 600 grams (21 ounces). At its point of release, a javelin may be moving at 113 km/h (70 mph)! A legitimate landing zone extends in a sector of 28.96 degrees from the launch arc. No unorthodox throwing style is permitted in official competition. After Uwe Hohn tossed the javelin 104.80 meters in 1984 and Petra Falke covered 80.00 meters in 1988, pushing the boundaries of competitive stadia, javelins were re-designed to fly in more of an arc, avoiding flat landings and shortening their carry; since then, the men's record was set at 98.48 meters by Jan Zelezny in 1996, and the women's mark set by Barbara Spotakova at 72.28 meters in 2008.

Long Jump

Run fast. Jump as far as you can. Land without hurting yourself—or falling backwards. That's about it for the long jump. Well, there are the limitations of the runway, the need to take off without overstepping the wooden board (or else a foul cancels that effort), and fighting the irrepressible force of gravity for as long as you can. The target—a rectangular box of sand within which to land—is made for the event. But you better hit just right, touching your shoes down at the last split-second with enough forward momentum to walk or fall forward of your landing spot. Elite jumpers customarily take 20-22 strides on their approach, then take off using a kick, double-arm, sprint, or power sprint style as they launch themselves into a hang, sail, or hitch-kick style of flight. Technique matters! Priorities are forward speed and take-off angle (ideally 20 degrees or less). Galina Chistyakova leapt a distance of 7.52 meters (24' 8") in 1988; Mike Powell propelled himself a record 8.95 meters (29' 4 1/4") in 1991.

Pole Vault

Back to the high jump we go. But this time, the bar is even higher; the intermediate goals are more demanding; and proper form is at an even higher premium, with the risk of injury heightened by the potentially longer fall. The pole is between 10 feet and 17' 4 1/2" long and customarily constructed of fiberglass. The competitor must run, typically in 18-22 strides, toward the high bar with that awkward implement in hand, not only balancing it but preparing to stick its end precisely into the plant box to begin the vault. Proper take-off is dependent upon exact timing and aim at that first target. The vaulter can then swing up with propulsion delivered by the bending pole, extend toward and over the primary target (the crossbar), turn, and fly away from the pole and bar (without knocking it down) en route to the landing pit below. How far below? Renaud Lavillenie set the men's record of 6.16 meters (20' 2 1/2") in 2014, while Yelena Isinbayeva raised her body over the crossbar at 5.06 meters (16' 7") in 2009. That landing pit is the final, thickly cushioned target of the vaulter. A pole vaulter needs a well-practiced blend of speed, strength, agility, and precision.

Running

Running—a target sport? May a finish line be considered a target to hit, an end zone within which to score? And where is the athletic level of difficulty in doing something as natural, an action developed through all of human evolution, as running? Well, maybe it's a stretch. But competitive runners always have targets—meeting split times, beating a specific total time, defeating one's fellow runners, reaching the conclusion of the race in good form. And while the skill itself surely has natural components that are shared by countless humans, elite runners must train exceedingly hard for speed and/or endurance. The sport is challenging enough to require specialization: the best sprinters of 100 or 200 meters are never able to win the 10,000-meter run or 26-mile marathon. Road or track runners usually have little to worry about when it comes to their footfalls—unless they're in a pack of competitors whose feet might collide as they maneuver for position. But competitors in the 3000-meter steeplechase have some targets in the form of obstacles they must clear—four hurdles and one water jump to leap—each lap of the race; it helps to be able to hurdle with either leg first. Competitors in the men's and women's hurdles races, of course, have even more jumps on which to stay focused as they zoom down (men 110 meters, women 100 meters) or around (400 meters) the track. And cross-country or trail runners lack a track to attack: their eyes must instantaneously scan the path ahead to see where it's safe to plant one's foot. Each step must aim for a safe target so as to avoid turning one's ankle by stepping on a stone, stick, or uneven terrain. Length of stride, then, must also be flexible while running through natural environments. Who is likely to be the superior athlete—one with the obvious musculature to race the 100-meter dash, or the typically thin distance runner with the leg strength and stamina to run the 26-mile marathon? Perhaps it is the middle-distance runner with the blend of physique and endurance needed to race a mile.

SHOT PUT
Here's another sport requiring the athlete to hurl an object from a designated small space into a delineated larger one. That target space is fairly easy to hit. But, of course, the distance covered

by the 16.01–pound shot (males) or 8.8–pound shot (females) determines who wins and loses. Proper throwing form, in either spin or glide style, must be cultivated and over-learned in order to ensure a strong toss without crossing the foul line (10-centimeter-high stopboard). Spinning generates rotational speed and power; the glide entails a strong kick to the front of the 7-foot diameter throwing circle. Must successful competitors in this specialized event require bulk and large muscles, balance and explosive force, in order to prevail. Records were not kept of how far ancestors of modern shot-putters tossed cannonballs. But current distance standards are 23.12 meters (75' 10") by Randy Bowers, and 22.63 meters (74' 2.75") by Natalya Lisovskaya.

Triple Jump

If the long jump sounds like a simple target game, maybe it is—compared to this twist on the same concept. It's time to run and take off into space again, defying gravity for as long and far as one can. But this time the competitor must hop, skip, and jump distances up to 60 feet for men (18.29 meters by Jonathan Edwards) and 50 feet 10 inches (15.5 meters by Inessa Kravets) for women; 1995 was a good year for self-propulsion through space. After one's sprint to the take-off, coordination skills must be continuous and fully synchronized with the demands of each of the three launch points; ideally, each phase is progressively higher.

Badminton

This racquet sport generates the most speed of any sport. The target, the birdie or shuttlecock, travels up to 206 miles per hour when first struck by a player. The shuttlecock's feathery construction causes it to slow down, but the opposing player must still move rapidly, reflexively to return a shot and, naturally, strive to be mindful of where to direct his or her counterattack. Each half of a regulation badminton court measures 6.7 by 5.18 meters (22 x 17 feet) for singles, so there is much ground to cover; the court is naturally wider, 6.1 meters or 20 feet, for doubles competition. Action is fast in this dynamic sport, often dominated by players from Asia and Europe.

Basketball

The American team was dominant for many years, but other country's squads improved significantly over time. The USA then turned to its professional players to bolster, and basically supplant, its best amateur players in order to regain modern dominance. The NBA remains the pre-eminent collection of basketball players on the planet, but numerous international teams and individuals have closed the gap. With teams playing for national pride and patriotism, along with the prestige of the Olympics, spirited competition is the rule rather than the exception every four years.

Boxing

Is the age-old sport of pugilism a targeted contest? Yes, indeed, it is. Judges observe closely as combatants launch gloved fists at one another, and count only specified contacts in the scoring. Only clean punches to the torso and head are scored in Olympic boxing; punches below the belt bring discredit. Defense is as important as offense since one's conscious well-being may depend on an effective block, deflection, or evasion; thus, the punches of one's opponent constitute fast-moving targets for intervention. In professional boxing, landed punches count but may not be as conscientiously counted in the relatively subjective scoring of a bout in which knockdowns and knockouts are the most valued goals. Bodily target areas are broad, but boxers typically aim to hit the face or abdominal region.

Boxing may be defined as a manly sport—one that is now contested by women, as well. In any event, it can be brutal and bloody. Subtlety and nuance take a backseat to overt aggression and hurtful contact. Ouch! Lasting damage to body and mind is an occupational hazard.

Canoe Slalom

Here's a water sport with free-flowing targets. Well, not exactly. Boulders and other rocky obstacles do not move, but the water that ebbs and rushes around them, influencing the direction of watercraft in them, makes their avoidance a fluid process. Canoe and kayak competitors race against the clock, but they must paddle a prescribed course past targets that demand their full attention and skill. 18-24 hanging gates adorn 300 meters of whitewater. Men compete in 3 classes: kayak, single canoe, and/or double canoe; women may engage in the first two of those competitions. Their boats have been aided greatly over time by technological developments that produce carbon fiber, kevlar, fiberglass, or epoxy resin watercraft. Dimensions are regulated, however, with the boats weighing at least 8 kilograms (20 pounds), stretching

350 centimeters (11 feet), and being 60 centimeters (2 feet) wide. The fastest time through the gates wins the race, and it's not easy. The swirling waters and raging currents make it impossible to take dead aim on the targets; one must maneuver and adapt to the flow of the course with strength and accuracy. Touching a gate adds 2 seconds to your time; missing a gate incurs a 50-second penalty. Capsizing prompts a swift rescue by support staff.

Canoe Sprint is another Olympic event contested over a straight, calm course of separate race lanes. Again, there are races for both men and women, canoes and kayaks, ranging from 200 to 1000 meters in length. I'll omit details here, though, since the targets of such races are simply keeping one's boat in its lane and crossing the finish line ahead of the other paddlers.

Decathlon

A jack of all trades and master of all is a champion decathlete. Competition is split into two days to give all entrants time to take part and to enable them some rest between these challenging events. Men compete against one another and strive to earn points for time and distance standards in the 100-meter dash, long jump, shot put, high jump, and 400-meter run the first day. They conclude with the 110-meter hurdles, discus throw, pole vault, javelin throw, and the climactic 1500-meter race. Physical skills and stamina, all-around athleticism, and intermittent mental focus are the attributes needed to emerge triumphant. (Women compete in their own slightly-modified version of the decathlon, but not yet at the Olympics.)

Diving

Diving into water—a target sport? How can leaping into the air warrant that designation? It does not matter which air or water molecules you hit along the way. Then again… Diving requires precision. You must place each step on a board or platform just so, at a measured pace, in order to launch yourself with optimal spring. Judges subtract points for dives that occur off-center, or too far, from the board or platform. And woe to he or she who stays too close to the launch pad, hitting it with any body part during execution of the dive. The surface of the water is surely a target. A spinning, gyrating, accelerating diver must spot the water just in time to straighten her body and plunge vertically into its depths, hands positioned in the manner that causes the smallest splash. In reality, each airborne movement is a target—tuck, pike, free, or layout position, each somersault or twist must be done fully with arms and legs, fingers and toes, head and torso in just the right space at the right time. Off the 10-meter platform, divers move at 30-35 mph as they near the surface of the water. It takes an ideal blending of power and grace, with an exquisite sense of pace and space, to do complicated aerial maneuvers and land exactly right.

Equestrian

When competitors are horsing around, are they aiming at targets? Yes, they are in many respects. There are multiple targets, along with much difficulty and danger, in the three equestrian events: dressage, show jumping, and three-day eventing. Each of those disciplines is contested in both individual and team competitions.

In the dressage competition, horses are expected to engage in extravagant, elegant, exquisitely executed movements in precise locations within the riding ring (which is dotted with alphabetical guideposts). The dressage rider must smoothly transition the animal's gaits among "free" and "collected" walks, as well as "collected" and "extended" trots and canters. Small circles are trotted slowly, 8-meter circles are done at a canter, while that faster pace must also be maintained doing figure-eights with flying lead changes. High-stepping, diagonal-moving gaits are featured, including special techniques such as piaffe, passage, pirouette, half-pass, renvers, and tempi changes. Judges award points for the purity of gaits and quality transitions on a 1-10 scale; they deduct for any error they perceive.

Horses and riders that compete in the show jumping arena must leap over single, double, and triple bars as high as 2 meters (6' 6") in height. There is typically a water jump, with a low hedge or fence at the leading edge of a pool up to 4.5 meters (14.9 feet) wide, along the 500-600-meter course. The rider needs to navigate multiple changes in direction along the way and her horse must respond readily to that rider's posture and focus to turn toward each path. The human and equine competitors strive for clearance over all of those targets for a clean, penalty-free ride.

Eventing athletes begin with a display of dressage skills that is somewhat less complex and demanding than that of the specific dressage competition. The second day, eventers run the cross-country course—a lengthy, up-and-down journey littered with as many as 40 obstacles to jump over. These logs, stones, railroad ties, and other targets are constructed of natural materials, up to

1.2 meters (4 feet) high, that suit the terrain. Some are placed on upward or downward slopes, some around turns, and often two border a shallow pond which the horses must leap into and traverse before jumping out. If a horse refuses to jump, or goes around an obstacle, penalty points accrue; if the animal crashes into the obstacle or slams on its brakes, the rider may go flying head-first toward a visit to the hospital. Time limits dictate the pace of attack of the cross-country course.

On the third day of eventing, show jumping is required. The jumps on the course are not as high as those of the specific show jumping event, but the horses and their riders must overcome fatigue that can be mounting from the first two days of competition. Concentration, courage, and endurance count. Eventing is not for the timid.

In most sports, body control is a worthy goal. Riding a horse, one's physical strength and centering ability is further taxed by the need to steer, brake, and generally control the body of the large animal on which one sits.

Gymnastics

Highly popular with spectators and challenging to the athletes are the individual and all-around gymnastics events. One look at the physique of a high-level gymnast and you know that their sport requires strength and fitness; watch the events and you'll see the elements of speed, agility, flexibility, and stamina, as well. Men compete in floor exercise, horizontal bar, parallel bars, pommel horse, rings, and vault; women compete in balance beam, floor exercise, uneven bars, and vault. In what ways may these events be construed to have targets toward which to aim?

The exercise floor has boundaries which may not be crossed without penalty, yet gymnasts push those limits in order to pack as many leaps, somersaults, twists, and dance moves as possible into each routine. Every time they leap into the air, they try to "stick" the landing in a balanced, still posture. The vault entails running full-speed down a runway, leaping upon a small springboard just right, and extending arms and body to the vaulting horse in order to propel oneself into the air for a high-speed series of aerial somersaults and twists before landing as solidly as possible on the mat ahead. Awareness of the three targets—springboard, vaulting horse, and mat—must be rapid but sure. The balance beam is a target unto itself; women must mount it and stay centered upon it through a series of turns, leaps, and ballet moves before dismounting from it and sticking the landing exactly right. Upon the uneven parallel bars, one higher than the other, female athletes target both bars for their spinning and twisting maneuvers, letting go of one bar to move to the other without losing grip or momentum. Men have just one bar of which to keep track, but it's high enough to enable the gymnast to circle it, release from it to do an acrobatic move, and recapture one's grip. You must keep close tabs on the bar—and the floor—while clutching it with both hands or only one at a time en route to a climactic take-off, aerial maneuver, and landing. The parallel bars and pommel horse exercises require amazing strength and focus on the apparatus under hand; the athlete creates powerful yet graceful moves from one section of the apparatus to another before, yet again, launching into a complicated release and centered landing.

Men strive to hang from the "still" rings—which are anything but stationary—with strength and control; handstands, somersaults, and the always-amazing "iron cross" abound before the gymnast can target the mat below for the big finish.

Sure, the targets seem secondary to the athletic skills and aerial maneuvers. But those are always centered around the apparatus being used; unplanned loss of contact with that equipment at any point of one's routine, before the finishing flourish, spells penalty point deductions and perhaps potential injury. Interestingly, during the span of Olympic competition 1896-2012, the most gymnastics medals by far have been won by the Soviet Union (URS), with the USA and Japan also head and shoulders above the rest of the nations of the world.

Handball

This variation of many other court sports is often referred to as team handball since the Olympic version entails teams of 7 players each—6 outfield players and 1 goalie. They compete for two 30-minute periods on an indoor court measuring 40 by 20 meters (131 by 66 feet). The rectangular goal stands 3 meters wide and 2 meters high; it's surrounded by a relatively large 6-meter, semi-circular zone, or crease, within which only the goalkeeper is permitted. There is an exception to that: an attacking player may leap from outside into the crease in the process of shooting at the goal, as long as that player's feet do not touch the court before releasing the ball. The ball is spherical and made of leather or synthetic material; men compete with a bigger ball (circumference of 58-60 centimeters weighing 425-475 grams) than do women (circumference of 54-56 centimeters weighing 325-375 grams). Field players may touch the ball with any body part above and including the knee. They may stand holding the ball for no more than 3 seconds, however, and take no more than 3 steps with it, before having to shoot, pass, or dribble (bounce) it. Otherwise, it's a turnover. This is somewhat of a contact sport; defenders may collide with an opponent's body if they actively try to steal or block the ball. They may only direct their actions at the ball; holding, pushing, hitting, tripping, jumping into, or reaching around an opponent is penalized by the two referees who monitor the game action. Bodily contact from the side or behind is also disallowed. Offensive and defensive strategies abound, making this a complicated sport. Handball has rules and strategies too complex and numerous to mention here, yet it is a relatively high-scoring endeavor with each team often tallying between 20 and 35 goals per game. There is plenty of action!

HEPTATHLON

The distaff version of all-around athletic competition consists of the following seven events: 100-meter hurdles, high jump, shot put, 200-meter run, long jump, javelin throw, and the concluding 800-meter race. As in the men's decathlon, competitors may target one another in each event but with the main focus on individual accumulation of points toward total score. American Jackie Joyner-Kersee holds the record for the highest score and is the only two-time Olympic gold medalist.

Judo
Men against men and women against women, seven weight classes of each battle on the mats. Judo means "way of suppleness", often characterized by giving and yielding in order to lure an opponent off-balance; it sounds like one's target is a non-target in the inscrutable manner of an Oriental discipline. But the 4-minute women's bouts and 5-minute men's bouts are physically demanding. The goal is to throw one's adversary to the floor and either immobilize him/her or force a submission. Three different scores are possible: (1) Yuko = take opponent down to the floor on his/her side and hold him/her there for at least 10 seconds; (2) Wazari = take the opponent to the floor, not on his/her back, and immobilize for at least 15 seconds; two Wazaris constitute an Ippon which is (3) a perfectly victorious throw, putting the opponent on his/her back on the floor, holding on for at least 20 seconds or making the adversary submit via an arm-lock or stranglehold. Combatants may not punch, kick, hold a belt, or evade contact (a lack of combativeness), as regulated by a referee. Which nation has won the most medals in this sport of Japanese origin? Japan, of course!

Modern Pentathlon
Here's a challenging skill set to test one's mettle. Competitors engage in a round-robin fencing tournament, facing every other opponent once. Score a single hit with your epee and you earn a point for winning that match; if neither contestant scores within a minute, both lose. Then it's time to follow the acts of swordmanship with a plunge into the swimming pool for a 200-meter freestyle race. Next comes show jumping in a unique format;

each athlete is randomly assigned a horse 20 minutes before the riding competition begins. Unfamiliar with one another, horse and rider must negotiate a course of 350-450 meters in length that contains 12-15 obstacles over which to jump. Pistol shooting, followed by 3000 meters of cross-country running, traditionally rounded out this competition—until recently, that is. Since 2013, modern pentathletes must shoot a laser pistol until they hit 5 targets (or 50 seconds elapse) before running 800 meters; and they must repeat that sequence 3 more times! Whoever hits 4 x 5 = 20 bull's eyes, and races 4 x 800 = 3200 meters, in the fastest time, wins. Seedings for that final, combined event must be based upon the results of the first three events. A modern pentathlete surely needs to hone a disparate set of gross and fine motor abilities, with stamina and horse sense to spare. Whichever man and woman cross the finish line first should be rightly proud of his/her multi-modal victory.

Rhythmic Gymnastics

These variations on gymnastics incorporate some of the strength, agility, balance, grace, and power of the regular gymnastics events, but typically add more elements of graceful dance to the athletic displays. Contested by females only are events utilizing props: clubs, hoop, ball, ribbon, and rope. Judges look for degree of difficulty of the leaps, balances, pirouettes, apparatus handling, and execution by the athletes, and assign an additional score for artistic impression. Routines are visually incredible to watch, mixing beauty and athletic prowess as they do, and the way that the competitors use their portable targets adds originality and aesthetic quality to each performance.

Rowing

The Olympic race course for all rowing events extends 2000 meters and accommodates six boats per heat. Both male and female competitors in sculling—single, double, and quadruple—handle two oars, one in each hand. Sweep events, in which each rower manipulates a single oar with both hands, include the coxless pair, coxless four (men only), and coxed eight (with a coxswain along for the ride to chant the pace that unifies the crew members). There are also lightweight events: double scull and coxless four for men, and double sculls for women. Athletes who row individually or compete in crew are typically well-proportioned muscularly, with strong legs valued at least as much as strong arms; watch rowers collapse over their oars in exhaustion at the conclusion of a race to gauge how much endurance is needed to compete successfully.

Rugby

American football is a rough sport. Players wear helmets, shoulder pads, knee pads, and assorted other protective gear under their uniforms, and still injuries abound. Now take that ruffian game and play a close semblance of it without any protective gear whatsoever. The ball is a little bigger and may be passed among teammates only backwards, never forward. But once it or the ball carrier hits the ground, the play is not over. Instead, one may pass the ball back along the ground to a teammate who may take up the running, carrying, and passing of the ball from there. Defenders tackle. Hard. Scoring in football and rugby are similar: a football "touchdown" earns six points and a point-after kick earns one extra (with a two-point conversion as an option), while a rugby player could cross the goal line for a five-point "try" and add two more points by drop-kicking the ball through the uprights.

Sailing

Cruising around a bay by the whim of the wind a highly competitive target sport under the Olympic banner? Sure, why not? Capricious winds meet technical development and tactical skills to propel boats of different sizes and styles 2-4 laps around a course specified by buoys. Those targets are evident; so are the other boats with which to contend but not collide. Men compete in five events, their classes being Laser, Finn, 470, 49er, and RS:X; the first two and last one are singles events, while the third and fourth classes are sailed by two men. Two women guide their 470 and 49er FX watercraft around the course, while individuals sail the Laser Radial and RS:X styles. There is one mixed event; a guy and a gal captain their Nacra 17 on the open water. Sailors must be totally attentive and ready to adjust their sails and use their weight quickly according to changing circumstances.

Shooting

There's no debating whether or not shooting is a target sport. And pairing weapons with targets is clearly a passionate pastime at the Olympic Games since no fewer than 9 events for men, and 6 for women, grace the program. Men shoot .177-inch pellets 60 times at targets 10 meters away using air pistols or air rifles. .22 caliber pistols are used for the 60 shots of the 50-meter pistol competition and the 60 shots, at 25 meters, using a rapid fire pistol. Also at a range of 50 meters are the .22-caliber rifle prone (60 shots), and rifle three positions (prone, kneeling, and standing, 3 x 40 shots), competitions. The male events are rounded out with the shotgun events of skeet (125 targets), trap (125 targets), and double trap (150 targets). Women also pick up their shotguns to shoot skeet and trap, with 75 targets each. The distaff competitors also take their turns with the air pistol (40 shots), air rifle (40 shots), pistol (30 + 30 shots), and rifle in three positions (3 x 20 shots). Perfect scores are rarely, if ever, achieved in these challenging events. Steady, focus, squeeze the trigger...

Swimming

Swimmers race against time, and one another, from wall-to-wall in pools and from the start to the finish line in open-water competitions. The sport requires fitness, skill, coordination, and countless hours of conditioning. But where do targets enter the equation? There are targets virtually every stroke of the way.

World-class swimmers are aware of every hand placement, reaching through air and breaching the surface of the water in the most aqua-dynamic manner possible. They remain mindful of the distance traveled, especially as they approach a wall for a turn. Flip too early and your leg extension barely touches the wall, the lack of push costing valuable chunks of time. Flip too late and you've gone farther than you needed to, have your legs scrunched too close to the wall for an efficient push, and even risk banging your heels on the side of the pool. During the final lap of a race, of course, the finish wall takes on added target value. Events are often decided by hundredths of a second, so a racer wants to remain streamlined every inch of the way while pushing through the strain and exhaustion that can cause one's muscles to tense, posture to lapse, head to move out of alignment, and timing of the final stroke to go awry. Lane lines help you to stay on target, in the center of that space, so as to minimize the distance covered and avoid a costly, time-consuming collision with those lines. Rules regarding underwater recovery---i.e., how far one may cruise underwater using a dolphin kick after each backstroke or butterfly start and turn---set up the need to be aware of that distance target. Distance swimmers pace themselves with targets—e.g., interval times, number of strokes per lap. Relay racers strive to be keenly aware, each starting his dive precisely so his toes leave the starting block exactly when his approaching teammate touches the wall. Other swimmers serve as targets, too, as a racer may hang just behind a competitor in the next lane to "draft" off his wake (beside the lane line between them) until it's time to make a move for the lead. So, the targets of a competitive swimmer are not as explicit as those of many other athletes; but they have them.

Synchronized Swimming

This female-only competition (with apologies to Bill May, a tremendous talent in the sport) requires tremendous grace, strength, stamina, and lung capacity. Duets and teams of eight perform pool-based gymnastics, dance, and swimming choreographed to music (pumped by speakers both within and outside the water). Actions must be exquisitely in unison or sequenced to impress the two panels of five judges, one group rating technical merit and the other judging artistic impression and capabilities. Each pair performs a technical routine, containing compulsory moves, for 2'

20", and then a free routine (with few restrictions) for 4 minutes; the octet does their technical routine for 2' 50". So precise and demanding are the arts that a head referee, clerical staff, back-up judges, and sound center manager help to monitor and regulate the proceedings. To what extent are targets involved? Nobody is shooting at anything, but partners may be considered objects of great scrutiny of one another in order to coordinate their movements in and above the water, in time to the music, in complete harmony. Each precise maneuver is a target at which to aim.

Table Tennis

"Unsound Condition" by Richard Armour:

> They're checking the Ping-Pong ball,
> For something, it seems, is wrong.
> It pongs when it ought to ping
> And it pings when it ought to pong.

I've played basement (or fraternity) ping pong most of my life. A silly refrain such as that one seems to fit my low-level expertise. But at the Olympic level, table tennis is an extremely fast-paced target sport. Competitors smash the hollow plastic ball back and forth at blinding speed (up to 70 mph), imparting topspin to such shots to guide them over the net onto the opponent's 137 by 152.5-centimeter portion of the table. Players also use chop, lob, and push (slice) shots, enhanced by backspin, sidespin, or cork spin, to distort the visual perception and quick reactions of their opponents. Each serve is a specialty shot, designed to get the ball into play and the other player slightly off-balance; it is kept low and spinning to prevent one's opponent from aggressively slamming home a point.

Ping pong, whether played purely for recreation at home, practiced competitively at a table tennis club, or contested at championship levels, is a wonderful life-long sport. Numerous health experts have touted it as one of the best athletic endeavors because of its blend of eye-hand coordination, reaction time, agility, and dexterity in a low-impact format. Injuries are uncommon. Perspiration is not.

Taekwondo

Any martial art entails anatomical targets. In the case of this Korean discipline, targets are strictly above the waist. "Tae" means "to stomp or trample", "kwon" refers to "fist", and "do" is a "way or discipline". Taekwondo, then, refers to "the way of the feet and hands". Both men and women compete in four weight classes: flyweight, featherweight, middleweight, and heavyweight. They spar for three rounds, with one-minute rests in between, engaging in full (rather than light) contact with the clock running continuously (rather than stopping in between points). One primary target is the torso; it is covered by a chest protector, or "hogu", that has recently been wired to score strikes electronically. Judges also rule the action, awarding 1 point for a regular kick or punch, and 2 or 3 points for a back or spinning kick, to the hogu. The superior target is the head. Any straight kick connecting with the head (also protected, by a soft helmet and a mouth guard) earns 3 points, while a turning or spinning head shot earns 4. (Note: scoring standards have been in flux in recent years as regulating organizations strive to add excitement to Olympic competition.)

Several techniques are taboo in taekwondo. Sparring opponents may not strike or block with the knee; grab, hold, or push one another; hit below the belt; punch the head; or attack a fallen opponent. Practitioners strive to embrace the "relax/strike principle": relax the body between blocks, kicks, and strikes, conserving and focusing energy and speed to tense the muscles while performing offensive and defensive techniques. (This is similar to a guiding principle of the Japanese art of aikido; overall relaxation is prized, tensing only those muscles just the right amount to execute a defensive maneuver.)

Tennis
This sport has already been profiled, of course. The lure of a potential gold medal in the Olympic Games attracts the most elite players in the world, perhaps as much as do the four Grand Slam events.

Trampolining
Bouncing on a trampoline can be fun. Backyards of many homes with children across America can attest to that. The sidewalls of most such trampolines imply the hazardous nature of bouncing on a springy, somewhat slippery surface. Not only could you bound off the trampoline toward the ground, but awkward landings upon the trampoline itself can be injurious, even crippling. So, trampoline athletes must stay focused upon the landing zone

as they launch into the acrobatics of competition: jumps (straight, tuck, pike, and straddle positions), somersaults, and twists. Olympic competitors get to do one quick warm-up jump before initiating their series of 10 tricky contacts; then one re-orienting "out bounce" is permitted before the final landing when the athlete and the bed of the trampoline must finish as motionless as possible. Athletic acumen, with a daredevil's attitude, best serve a competitive trampoliner.

Triathlon

A nominee for most talented all-around athlete is the triathlete. Olympic contestants do an open water swim of 1500 meters (1650 yards), transition onto their bicycles to race 40 kilometers (24.9 miles), and dismount in order to run 10 kilometers (6.2 miles). (Distances in the grueling Ironman Triathlon, incidentally, are 2.4 miles, 112 miles, and 26.2 miles, respectively.) Triathletes target specific split times while monitoring their fellow competitors and, probably, keeping track of their heart rates and physical well-being.

Volleyball

Six players per team roam the volleyball court that typically measures 9 x 18 meters (29.5 x 59 feet). Their task is to hit the ball, measuring 65-67 centimeters in diameter and weighing between 260 and 280 grams, no more than three times before launching it across the net to the opposing squad. The target, of course, is some space between the other team's members in order to score a point. With the net standing at 2.24 meters (7' 4 1/8") for women, and elevated to 2.43 meters (7' 11 5/8") for men, the sport tends to attract relatively tall players. Height and reach better enable one to block a slam or dink at the net, or to rocket a shot toward the opposition. But there are places for players of shorter stature. The "3-hit rule" gives a team the chance to set up the ball for the decisive blast over the net. As for beach volleyball, obviously played on sand and involving only two-person teams commanding a somewhat smaller court, the players' rules and roles are very much the same as those of the larger collegiate and Olympic sport.

Water Polo

Water polo presents it own unique set of challenges. Players rely on teamwork, swimming speed, ability to tread water in a pool typically 6.5-8 feet (at least 1.8 meters) deep, and sheer strength to succeed at throwing a ball into a net for a score. Opponents strive to block shots or steal the ball, sometimes using underwater tactics such as kicking, grabbing and pulling swimsuits, or trying to submerge their adversaries. Officials remain alert for any signs of fouls, but it's hard for them to detect the action that takes place under the churning water. Infractions range from minor fouls to brutality. Each of the six field players, along with the goalie, wear caps or head gear with protective ear coverings. The ball resembles a soccer ball, and its dimensions vary for men and women: the male version has a diameter of 22 centimeters, a circumference of 68-71 centimeters, and inflation pressure of 90-97 kPa (kilopascals or 13-14 psi); females compete with a ball with a diameter of 21 centimeters, circumference of 65-67 centimeters, and pressure of 83-90 kPa (12-13 psi). Goalkeepers protect targets that are 3 meters wide and 90 centimeters high. Shots on goal can reach speeds of 30-56 mph. Stamina is needed to play the four 8-minute periods that constitute a match. Treading water with an "eggbeater" kick, swimming rapidly back-and-forth across the expanse of water (30 x 20 meters for men, 25 x 20 meters for women), passing and shooting the ball within the confines of a 30-second shot clock, and engaging in physical conflict under and atop the water make this a grueling sport.

Weightlifting

The degree of difficulty and challenge is obvious: a competitor aims to lift nearly three times his or her body weight overhead. It takes strength, of course, and wikipedia.com adds that weightlifters need to psych themselves to be "dynamic and explosive while appearing graceful." Males and females alike compete in eight weight classes, the former ranging from 56 kilograms to 105 kg+, and the latter weighing 48 kg and perhaps exceeding 75 kg. Each gets three trials to conquer the target weight in two events: snatch (lifting the barbell from floor to overhead in a single movement) and/or clean & jerk (a two-stage lift from ground to shoulder height, then overhead with elbows locked out straight). The heavyweights have hoisted some heavy weights. Current world records in the snatch are 214 kilograms (472 pounds) by Behdad Salimi of Iran and 155 kg (342 pounds) by Tatiana Kashirina of Russia; Tatiana also holds the women's clean & jerk record of 193 kg (425 pounds), while her fellow Russian, Aleksey Lovchev, has gotten 264 kg (582 pounds) stationary over his head.

Wrestling (Freestyle & Greco-Roman)

The former allows a combatant to use any part of his/her body for moves, locks, holds, and takedowns, while the latter style restricts the wrestler to the use of arms and upper body for grappling. Both men and women compete in six weight classes of freestyle wrestling. Only men match up in six weight classes of Greco-Roman wrestling. What are the objectives? Holds and throws earn points, but the real target is putting your opponent's shoulders to the mat for a winning pin or fall. The other path to victory is gaining a 10-point advantage in freestyle, or an 8-point lead in Greco-Roman, to win the match by technical fall. The referee not only regulates the match but also calls the points and penalties. Those "anti-targets" include strikes with knees, eye-pokes, hair-pulls, and, naturally, strangulation. Those rules are enforced not only by the referee but also by a judge and a mat chairman seated just off the mat; three more "expert" judges sit nearby to adjudicate any challenges to rulings during a match. Wrestling involves <u>intense</u> exertion. Anatomical targets to grab in order to achieve leverage and take your opponent off-balance, or to undo her/his advantage, are fleeting. The athletes struggle for control over one another for two three-minute periods with only a 30-second break in between them.

CHAPTER 5

Winter Olympic Sports

• • •

THE FOLLOWING SELECTION OF SPORTS of the Winter Olympics, held every four years like their summer counterparts, have elements of target orientation (besides the medal podium) and their own special skills and challenges:

- Biathlon
- Bobsleigh, Luge, & Skeleton
- Curling
- Figure Skating
- Ice Hockey
- Skiing: Alpine, Freestyle, & Nordic
- Ski jumping & Nordic Combined
- Snowboarding
- Speed Skating (long and short track)

Many sports are played within a controlled climate. Some, such as football or rugby, are played in all sorts of weather conditions. Others are contested in variable weather, but may be postponed if things get too severe; baseball and softball games get rained out, golf tournaments get suspended in thunderstorms, and tennis players head for cover when rain intensifies. Some of these

Winter Olympic sports are played indoors—namely curling and speed skating—but the others are contested on snow or ice in what may be frigid temperatures or blizzard conditions.

Biathlon

Biathlon combines highly active cardiovascular exercise alternating with target shooting that demands steady aim; control of one's breathing and nerves is of paramount importance during the "breathers" one takes to fire a rifle with precision. The skiing is rigorous, up and down twisting terrain with the clock and fellow competitors pushing the pace. Transitions between the two domains must be taxing indeed. The skier must slow down efficiently, with lowered blood pressure, in order to shoot accurately before accelerating again onto the race course. What a challenging blend of gross and fine motor skills!

Bobsleigh, Luge, & Skeleton

Driving a sled down an icy track at high speed is exhilarating, competitive, and dangerous. Bobsleigh athletes must also have speed and power to get their two- or four-person sled underway at the top of the run; split-seconds count. Bobsleigh drivers and brakemen need specified skills and timing to help them negotiate twists and turns efficiently, striving to stay on the fastest track of the run. Feet-first luge athletes and head-first skeleton competitors also need to know what they're doing on the curvy speedway. Involvement of targets in these sports, however, seems minimal. As stated, the athletes must aim at certain places to adjust their steering to regulate their sleds through the corners, but sled technology and aerodynamic riding postures have a lot to do with the finish time at the finish line.

CURLING

Curling is surely a target sport, like playing shuffleboard on ice. On the surface, it looks easy, but it takes a host of athletic skills and sensitive "touch" to toss and guide your team's stones to outscore those of your opponents. Success at curling also requires superior strategy to knock or block the throws of the opposing team.

Curling actually uses stones, polished granite ones that weigh between 38 and 44 pounds (17-20 kilograms); their maximum circumference is 36 inches (910 millimeters) and their minimum height is 4.5 inches (110 millimeters). Only the running surface of the stone, a metal ring about 5 inches in diameter in the concave bottom of the stone, is in contact with the ice. Two teams of four, each member wearing one slider shoe and one gripper shoe, take turns launching stones down the curling sheet, a rectangular playing area 146-150 feet (45-46 meters) long and 14.5-16.5 feet (4.4-5.0 meters) wide. The target is a conventional-looking one of concentric rings with diameters of 4, 8, and 12 feet. There is space behind the target, which is 16 feet from the backboard, and 6 feet behind the outside ring is the hack—a stake for the stone thrower to use to push off against to propel the stone toward the target at the opposite end of the sheet. Here's where things get tricky, though. Using its handle, the thrower may impart spin to the stone; that turn or curl gives it a curved trajectory. Two teammates may then influence that path of the stone using curling brooms. They brush the ice just before the moving stone to adjust its speed, distance, and direction. The fourth member of the team stands behind the target area verbalizing feedback to the sweepers about how and when to intervene with their brooms. May one accidentally touch a moving stone with a brush? Heck no! That infraction removes that stone from play, and any stones it may have hit and moved are reset to their former positions on the ice.

Teams may try to block or knock their opponents' stones. They seek to score one point for each stone of theirs that is closer to the "button" (bull's eye) than any stone of the other squad. Thus one team scores between 1 and 4 points per round. Scottish emigrants took their sport to Canada, the country with which it seems most closely associated today. Separate men's and women's teams contest this icy chess match, with its apparent simplicity but complex rules and strategies.

Figure Skating

One of the headline events of any Winter Olympics is the figure skating, women's and men's. Individual competitions are augmented by coed pairs and ice dancing. Men's and women's singles events used to be heavily target-oriented, with compulsory figures (12 specified patterns skated by all athletes) accounting for 60% of total score until 1947; then the number of figures was reduced to 6 that still counted 60% in the scoring. In 1968, the scoring proportion between the compulsory and free skating portions went to 50/50, and a short program was introduced in 1973. In July, 1990, the compulsories were dropped altogether in favor of just the short program and the long program. Skaters now set their own targets—where, when, and how to leap, spin, and perform assorted stunts on the ice, either singly or in pairs. Obviously, the pairs and dance events favor synchronization of movements, in time with the music, to impress the judges. Skaters push the limits of their capabilities, often to the edge of falling (which they sometimes exceed), in order to emerge victorious.

Ice Hockey

This international Olympic competition, with its many challenges and targets, has already been described in detail among major league sports. Suffice it to say that national pride and the lure of Olympic medals intensify the competitiveness of participants to fever pitch.

Skiing

Alpine, or downhill, skiing requires strength, quick reflexes, and stamina. Many such race events are determined by the clock. But they have targets. Ski racers must navigate gates; some are far apart and taken at high speed, as in the downhill, while others are close together and require rapid, frequent, and precise turning, as in the slalom. The Super G and giant slalom events are somewhere in between. The combined event consists of one downhill and two slalom runs. Every ski race requires planning on a line of attack of the course in order to begin each turn, or initiate each pre-jump, advantageously. To follow the fall line and cut as close to gates as possible, obviously without striking them with any force, is the way to optimize one's speed and finishing time.

Ski racing takes power, agility, timing, and a daredevil spirit to succeed.

In recent Olympics, skiers have added freestyle events to their program. Ski cross pits four racers against one another simultaneously speeding down a hill that includes big-air jumps and high-banked turns, challenges that help separate the winners from the losers. Ski cross racers must stay aware of three targets at once: elements of the terrain, locations of fellow competitors, and the clock. Slopestyle skiers likewise approach targets that send them into the air and elicit a variety of stunts; they ride rails, take off from jumps, and face other terrain park features not to beat one another on the clock but to impress judges instead. Freestyle skiers race down courses of moguls that require rapid, pulse-pounding, knee-bouncing turns accompanied by a pair of jumps for aerial antics. Half-pipe and aerial competitions invite more fancy flying for judges to rate.

Ski Jumping

Ski jumping, on the 60- or 90-meter hill, is a straightforward proposition. Overall time matters little. No turns or vigorous ex-ertions are needed. Gravity does much of the work. The only targets are the take-offff and landing zones. But what a terrifying endeavor! That 60 mile-per-hour take-offff requires a well-timed lunge into perfect aerodynamic form to maximize loft and distance. After holding that form in the air, flying as far as 251.5 meters at a height of 10 or 15 feet above the contoured slope, the jumper must switch into balanced landing form just as she regains contact with the snow-covered surface below. World-class ski jumpers are slender, wiry strong, and fully composed. The cost of a bad landing can be steep.

Snowboarding

Snowboard racers also have designated courses within which they must stay during races. Like ski racers, they strive to choose their paths and turning points in conjunction with the fall line in order to prevail in a race. Unlike ski racers, however, snowboarders challenge slalom and giant slalom courses in "parallel" competition—i.e., head-to-head in pairs. The snowboard cross event doubles that, of course, just as ski cross includes four competitors at once. Jumps, beams, and other obstacles adorn the cross course, forcing the racers to use a variety of skills and strategies to prevail. Boarders, like skiers, also compete in slopestyle to show their range of dangerous, high-flying tricks to judges; terrain park features propel boarders into spins, flips, grabs, and grinds. Halfpipe competition, perhaps the highest-profile snowboard event, rounds out the Olympic agenda of these athletes. Risk-taking, flamboyance, and skill blend into the best performances worthy of medal consideration. Go off-target and, unfortunately, the resulting crash can result in injury as well as defeat.

Speed Skating

Speed skating may be short- or long-track. Races on the former include a group of six skaters who become targets for one another—to pass and beat to the finish line, or to nudge off-balance along the way. Strategy and timing play large roles in how and when to make one's move toward the lead of the pack.

And given the sharp curves of the small oval, each placement of one's skate must be carefully yet spontaneously targeted. Races may start slowly but crescendo toward exciting finishes.

On the big oval, skaters race the clock against only one opponent at a time, but that other skater serves as a target for one's attention and comparison. Those racers must switch places, between inner and outer ovals, during the event in order to even out the distance traveled; those transitions may benefit (via drafting) or harm (via near-collisions) each pair when it comes to the overall target, one's finishing time. Perfect form, minimal wind resistance, and proper pacing lead to positive race outcomes.

CHAPTER 6

Less Widespread Sports

• • •

HUMANS HAVE CREATED AND PLAYED sports and games of all sorts, some of which have gained popularity and some that remain esoteric and get played in relative obscurity. Here's a look at some historical and modern-day target games.

- Archery
- Chess Boxing
- Finger Jousting
- Frisbee Disc Golf
- Haggis Hurling
- Jai Alai
- Juggling
- Martial Arts
- Paddle Tennis
- Paintball
- Pickleball
- Platform Tennis
- Polo
- Roller Derby
- Trap & Skeet Shooting

Ultimate Frisbee
Unicycle Basketball
Unicycle Hockey

Archery

Here's a sport whose roots trace back to medieval, if not ancient, times (10,000-9,000 BC). Bows and arrows evolved over the centuries for hunting, battle, and recreation on a worldwide basis. Today, playing perhaps the most quintessential target game, target archers aim for the center of the target of concentric circles set at various distances in a wooded or field setting. Modern bows and arrows vary in design and composition. Shooting accurately is no easy skill; however, mechanical sights fixed to the longbow aid in aiming while compound bows and crossbows employ cams or elliptical wheels that reduce the amount of strength needed to draw the bowstring. Olympic competition is guided by strict parameters. For added challenge and variety, try "archery golf"; contestants shoot arrows into a series of holes, goals, or targets on a course. Of course, the fewest number of shots wins.

Chess Boxing

You guessed it: competitors alternate between the two truly disparate pursuits. Capture your target, the king, in the chess game, or take aim to knock out your opponent in the ring, and you're the winner of the match. The blend of intellectual and physical skills makes this sport an impressively difficult one.

Finger Jousting

Think of jousting. Now imagine that medieval pastime without horses, armor, and lances. Instead, place two contestants on foot in close proximity to one another—clasping right hands, in fact—and have them poke one another with their right index fingers in order to score points. Touches to the head earn 3 points; pokes of the torso, neck, or back deserve 2 points apiece; and one earns one point for each scoring poke to the arms or legs of one's adversary. Six points win the bout. But note that finger jousters must abide by five rules:

1) A player's left hand stays behind his back
2) She may not use her legs or feet to trip her opponent
3) Fingernails must be trimmed to proper length
4) You must respect your opponent; the groin is off-limits
5) Players must honor the outcome of their match

It may sound a little silly, but it takes skill and exertion to execute effectively. Look for it on YouTube; it may take a while to qualify as an Olympic sport.

Frisbee Disc Golf

Now here's a personal favorite. This ol' hippie must be well-suited for throwing the ol' Mars Platter through space, curving it around trees and other obstacles toward a basket goal. In the woods and over meadows, this game has ease and enjoyment written all over it. But isn't it surprising that the best players now carry full sets of Frisbee discs—varying diameters and weights, for specified distances, built to curve certain directions to certain degrees—to tackle the challenges that courses provide? Some holes are long and hence difficult to par. Mother Nature often provides plenty of defense in the way of trees and shrubs. Perhaps a stream, hill, or other natural obstacle complicates matters.

The target is reasonably large and visible—a metal mesh basket 26 inches in diameter with a depth of 7 inches, supported by a steel pole 66 inches in length. The central portion of the basket is suspended from a metal ring around the upper part of the pole by 18 chains that manage to expand the target area; a player typically aims at the chains which will drop the disc into the basket, rather than trying to loft the frisbee so that it drops cleanly into the basket. Big target or not, the game is challenging. Holes can be hundreds of yards in length, though they're typically shorter than that, and cannot be reached easily in one or two shots even by long-distance throwers. Add the aforementioned natural obstacles, wind, and some whimsical curves by airborne discs, and one's score can soar.

Haggis Hurling

Thank goodness, this particular pastime places less of a premium on accuracy than on distance. Still, one must make a toss within the parameters of the playing field. The first objective is to make sure that your haggis fits the acceptable criteria for the competition: your sheep heart, liver, or other innards must fit neatly inside the regulation sheep's bladder. You must have the eye, nose, and stomach for the sport.

Jai Alai

This Latin American version of sports such as racquetball or squash adds elements that make it fast-paced and hazardous. The ball (pelota) is whipped against a forward wall by a curved, hand-held basket-like launcher (cesta or basque pelota) at speeds up to 188 miles per hour. Injuries are common and even fatalities have been recorded. As in those other court sports, the ball must be caught before it bounces more than once on the floor. Players, therefore, aim for corners, low points, and other strategic locations as their targets. There is no right-hand wall, so all must play right-handed. The sport is popular in the Philippines and Florida, as well as Latin American countries, and has attracted gamblers who bet on the outcomes of matches.

Juggling

Is this a target sport? Anyone who has juggled for an hour—with balls, clubs, rings, and assorted paraphernalia—knows that it is good exercise. It develops strength, stamina, eye-hand coordination, and focus on targets. By oneself, tosses and catches require accuracy in order to keep objects in the air in competition with the relentless force of gravity. Passing and interacting with juggling partners steps up that need for accuracy, rapidly shifting attention, consistency, concentration, and group cohesion. The more on-target the passes, the better the chance of their being caught in rhythm by one's partner so as to enable continuation of the exchange.

Martial Arts

Practitioners of boxing, karate, tae kwon do, and kendo entail targets that are not only moving, and hence elusive, but that are simultaneously taking aim at <u>their</u> targets. Your opponent is trying to hit parts of your body even as you try to zero in on theirs. This dynamic reciprocity could make shooting at station-ary targets seem relatively easy. Amateur pugilists wear boxing gloves and headgear to soften the blows, but the sport remains brutal in the eyes (and concussed brains) of many. Professional fighters wear gloves, of course, but leave their heads exposed to attack. Karate means "empty hand", but the hands of expert karateka may be considered lethal weapons in and of themselves. Sparring matches in karate may involve minor or full contact, and the combatants aim for points of particular vulnerability. Taekwondo, using kicks more than hand strikes, has been dis-cussed in the context of the Olympics. Kendo practitioners use shinai—46-inch swords made of bamboo and suede that deliver a sting or wallop, but typically no lasting damage—to take aim at one another. Those weapons are potent enough, however, to justify the wearing of protective uniforms by contestants. Aikido masters and students toss one another onto the ground and/or pin them to the mat, but in non-injurious manner by design. Aikidoka have no targets; they defensively respond to whatever attack may be aimed at them in practice (or reality) sans any sparring or competition. There are additional schools of martial arts, of course, and training in them offers challenges as well as benefits to body, mind, and spirit.

Paddle Tennis
This variant of its parent game uses the same ball, but depressurized to make it go slower. The underhand serve and solid wood/composite paddle also decelerate the pace of action to suit the smaller court (20 by 50 feet). It's a target sport for young and old alike.

Paintball
Take aim on your friends and family with reasonably harmless globs of paint. Actually, the balls are typically gelatin capsules containing polyethylene glycol and dye. Since they explode on impact after being shot by a carbon dioxide-propelled paintball marker, or gun, participants must wear masks or goggles. Additional protective clothing is recommended. Leagues, tournaments, and an expanding number of facilities make this typically outdoor sport increasingly popular. People team up to compete in games such as (1) Woodsball (Bushball), obviously played in the woods, (2) MilSim (military simulation) involving mission planning, combat, and attainment of objectives, and (3) Speedball with inflatable "bunkers", contested on a flat-turf open field. Run for cover! When moving or stationary human targets are hit, they're out of the game (for that round anyway).

Pickleball
Does this sport involve hitting a ball at or with a pickle? Or does it use a green, knobby, oblong ball? Neither. Invented in 1965, it has become a popular game in all 50 states with 2.46 million players as of 2015. It's a paddle sport with elements of tennis,

badminton, ping pong, and racquetball. On a court 20 by 44 feet (for singles or doubles, about the dimensions of a badminton court) is a net 36 inches high at the sidelines and 34 inches in the center. Players use composite paddles to whack a plastic ball that travels about one third the speed of a tennis ball. That reduced rate makes this sport less challenging than its faster-paced cousins and entices more aging participants than elite athletes in their prime.

Platform Tennis

Another modified version of tennis? Yes, and this time on a smaller court that is fenced by taut chicken wire off which shots may be played. The solid sponge rubber ball and overhead serve enable some speedy exchanges and odd bounces, the play thus resembling that of racquetball or squash.

Polo

This sport resembles a cross between croquet and field hockey---except for the minor complication that it's played on horseback instead of on foot. Each skilled rider needs a stable of talented, well-trained horses to compete effectively in the polo arena. With all of the starts and stops, precarious twists and turns, and high-speed running, horses tire quickly and need replacement. Passing among teammates, playing group strategy, defending against the opposing team, swinging to strike a stationary or moving ball down on the ground, all the while trying not to collide injuriously with friend and foe alike, make this multi-dimensional sport an obviously taxing one.

Playing polo is not for the faint-hearted or financially insecure. Both people and horses face potential injury. Polo ponies are a breed unto themselves, bred and trained for this specialized sport. A good horse costs a pretty penny.

Polo is usually contested on a grass field up to 300 yards (274 meters) long and 160 yards (146 meters) wide. Four players per team play 4-8 seven-minute periods called chukkas; they get four minutes of rest between chukkas with a ten-minute halftime break during which spectators get a chance to engage in divot stomping to level the playing field, literally. The primary rule of the sport entails "line of the ball": a player who strikes the solid plastic ball along a certain trajectory has the right of way to continue along that path; direct interference by an opponent is a foul. Furthermore, an opponent may not purposely touch another player, tack, or pony with the lengthy wooden mallet. The opponent may, however, intrude indirectly by riding up alongside a player on line with the ball and either make shoulder-to-shoulder contact, hook that player's mallet, bump his horse, push him off line, or steal the ball. Atop 1200-pound animals, these actions are bound to make this a rough sport!

But if polo sounds too tame and elitist, consider playing a variation on the theme. In winter, snow polo ponies may be guided on compacted snow fields or frozen lakes, three players per team striving to score goals with a brightly colored, lightweight plastic ball. Other fair-weather versions of the sport may be played in canoes or automobiles, atop motorcycles or bicycles, driving golf carts, or "riding" hobby horses. Where available, polo players may eschew speedy, agile horses to ride camels, elephants, or yaks instead. Yikes!

Roller derby

Here's a sport that's undergoing a resurgence of popularity. Just check for it online. Once an oft-televised professional women's sport (about 50 years ago), it is now being played by a plethora of amateur teams from coast-to-coast. Teams of five hit the oval track on conventional, four-wheeled roller skates. Round and round they go. A designated "jammer" from each team tries to lap the field and make her way through the four "blockers" of the opposing squad, scoring a point for each person thus passed. Her teammates can help open the way, if possible, with hips checking and elbows flying. Rules are enforced and penalties applied—it's not a violent free-for-all—but it's a rough sport requiring skill and agility on skates en route to the target of making one's way through the entire pack of skaters. Men's teams are starting to proliferate, still outnumbered by the females on the rink but serving as testimony to the skill, fun, and athleticism showcased by this sport.

Trap & skeet shooting

Shooting a rifle at a stationary target is plenty hard. This sport demands one to hit moving targets, but offsets some of that difficulty through the use of shotguns. The scattered, spherical pellets (lead shot #7.5 to #9, 2.0-2.4 millimeters in diameter) are far more likely to break a clay pigeon than is a single rifle bullet. Trap shooters typically use single- or double-barreled 12-gauge shotguns to aim at clay pigeons rising and going away at different angles, launched from a single "house" (machine housed in a small shed). Skeet shooting has more crossing and some double targets, launched on sideways paths from two houses. Even more challenging (and expensive) is sporting clays: marksmen walk through woods to different stations where target clays are propelled in various directions. Semi-automatic shotguns make the sport more rapid-fire.

Olympic Trap, cited earlier, began in 1900, with the current version inserted into the Games in 1950. Double Trap began in 1996, for men only, demanding shots to destroy two targets thrown simultaneously at slightly different angles. Back in 1995, Commander Mike Piffle achieved a famous "eighteen in eighteen" by using 18 shots in 18 seconds to hit all double clays from a distance of 60 meters. Kim Rhode, a female four-time Olympian, won the gold medal in 2012 by hitting 99 of 100 clays. Most amateurs cannot approach those levels of accuracy, with trap shooting rated as relatively easiest at which to achieve competence.

Ultimate Frisbee

Playing catch with a friend with a Frisbee can be highly enjoyable. It's fun to do so on the run. This game merely takes that basic activity, adds teammates and opponents, and gives guidelines that make the game into a cross between football and basketball. Players may guard one another, striving to block or steal passes, while other defenders try to intercept passes in flight or cause a fumble (dropped or errant pass) that prompts a change of possession. You must be fairly adept at throwing the disc with a forehand motion, in addition to the more traditional backhand release, and be able to "see" your teammate's evolving path in order to lead him or her with an accurate pass. If wind and rain affect the flight of a football, you can imagine how inclement weather can make throwing and catching Frisbees even more difficult; after all, they're lightweight, spinning circles that are dependent on air for their lift, carry, and directionality. Long throws and spectacular diving catches enhance the visual appeal and adventure of this sport.

Unicycle Basketball

Basketball is a demanding sport as it's traditionally played. Unicycling is a talent all by itself; it requires amazing balance, concentration, and reflexes to stay aboard and move in a desired direction. Idling a unicycle—staying relatively in one place—is a specialized skill that comes in handy on a basketball court where one is trying to cover an opposing player and change direction in sync with him. Dribbling, passing, and shooting a basketball from the elevated, unstable seat of a unicycle must be truly difficult to do. Possession is awarded to the other team if the ball handler travels (three half-turns of the wheel without dribbling), stays in the key for four seconds, or slides off his unicycle. Even free throws are shot from one's unicycle seat. Shooting percentages are sure to suffer as a result.

Most players choose unicycles with wheels that are 24 inches in diameter; some play with 20-inch-diameter wheels, sacrificing some height and speed for greater maneuverability. Plastic (rather than metal) pedals are a must in order to protect players' shins. Some participants wear shin and/or ankle guards. Player-to-player physical contact is, thankfully, minimal.

Unicycle Hockey

Unicycles on ice??? Luckily, no. This non-contact version of ice hockey has rules similar to its parent sport, but the competitors usually roll on unfrozen surfaces and hit a tennis ball with their ice hockey sticks. It resembles inline or roller skate (street, parking lot) hockey but with the added skill component of balancing and moving with agility on a unicycle.

Which target games have I yet to mention? Have I left out the energetic, fast-moving court games of racquetball and squash? Olympic battles in judo, taekwondo, and boxing have now been joined by amateurs and professionals who risk injury in the more brutal, less rule-bound matches in mixed martial arts (MMA). I have also neglected to cite numerous other types of events covered by sports media. Motorsports have huge followings because their drivers need skill, strength, and coordination to navigate their vehicles over tracks and race courses of various types, usually at dangerous speeds. Jockeys are typically diminutive but wiry-strong individuals who guide racehorses at thundering velocity. Whether racing on the flats or over the obstacles of a steeplechase, those riders face serious challenges and the risk of injurious falls off their horses; the horses face danger, too, with approximately 1.6 per 1000 runners euthanized due to race injury. Bicyclists race on roads and tracks, on flat and mountainous terrain, with the risk of crashes adding the element of danger to every type of contest. Members of cheerleading teams perform targeted routines featuring impressive feats of athleticism and synchronization. Sportsmen go after moving targets; some hunt with rifles to shoot natural prey while others fish with poles and bait to catch aquatic animals. Our sports networks also cover competitive eating (hot dogs), spelling, and poker playing contests—competitive endeavors that don't quite qualify as athletic accomplishments keyed in on targets.

CHAPTER 7
Games

• • •

NOT ALL TARGET GAMES REQUIRE substantial degrees of athletic endowment. Some are much more tame, with minimal cardiovascular exertion needed to play. As opposed to sports, games may be played with limited movement and reduced need for muscular development, agility, gross motor coordination, speed, and stamina. However, games such as the following require eye-hand coordination and include admirable degrees of difficulty.

- Billiards
- Bocce
- Croquet
- Darts
- Foosball
- Horseshoes
- Lawn Bowling
- Marbles
- Quoits
- Shuffleboard
- Snooker
- Tiddlywinks

Billiards

Down to a smaller scale compared to field sports like baseball, football, and soccer, and arena sports such as tennis, it must be simple to play pocket billiards. Using a table with dimensions of 4 x 8 feet, the magnitude of the game is easy to grasp visually compared to other sports. Spectators stay quiet and fellow competitors do nothing to interfere with one's shooting. Well, that is unless one's opponent intentionally leaves the cue ball squarely behind the proverbial, or actual, 8-ball. Calm nerves, steady hands, and skilled eye-hand coordination must combine with visual foresight and geometric angle perception to make any given shot. But to excel, one must plan and control, using "English", ricochet, and touch, where the cue ball will come to rest in preparation for the succeeding string of shots.

Bocce

Bocce is a sport contested by old men and women, right? Not according to its national governing body, the United States Bocce Federation (USBF). People of all ages may play and compete in the traditional Volo style or the more modern Raffa style; world championships in those styles were first held in 1947 and 1983, respectively. A typical bocce court consists of a layer of clay atop gravel. It measures between 76 and 90 feet in length and has a width from 10 to 12 feet. A Volo court has no sideboards, while a Raffa court is flanked by treated lumber 10 inches high. Each player has four spheres to toss in the direction of the target jack. Volo balls are made of bronze, weigh 2-2.6 pounds apiece, and are 3.5-4.3 inches in diameter; Raffa competitors use plastic balls weighing 2 pounds with a diameter of 4.2 inches.

The first player tosses the jack, or wooden pallino (diameter 1.4 inches), onto the court. The players begin by taking a toss at the jack. Whoever ball is closest to it continues to throw as long as his/her tosses are closer than the one of the opponent; if a toss is farther away, the turn changes. After each has tossed all four spheres, the score depends on how many balls are closer to the jack than any of the opponent's tosses. Thus, the closest earns one point; if that player also has the second closest result, two points are awarded (and so on). Should disputes occur or rules need discussion, Raffa players rely upon a referee while Volo adherents referee themselves. Games usually last somewhere between 7 and 13 points.

Is bocce an easy game to play? Its physical demands are small. The strategy is relatively uncomplicated. But it takes good aim and touch to toss balls close to the target, perhaps knocking aside opponents' balls or blocking the path to the target effectively.

CROQUET

This gentle art is often associated with settings of wealth and leisure. It's a game that requires little physical exertion or athletic skill to execute, though there are skills to acquire via time and practice. One needs eye-hand coordination and touch to swing the hammer to direct the wooden ball through one or more wickets per shot. Although the end post is a stationary, point-scoring target, there are times when it pays to aim at the ball of an opponent to knock it off-course. A cutthroat attitude can pay dividends.

Darts

The genteel game of darts is accomplished by directing sharp objects (typically weighing about 20 ounces and aerodynamically designed) at a target board 18 inches in diameter from a distance of 7 feet, 9.25 inches (2.37 meters). That distance, from the oche (or throwing line) to the target, may vary between 7' 6" to 9', depending upon the pub or game room in which you play. But the center bull, or bull's eye, should always be 5' 8" from the floor. Such humble dimensions should make for an easy game, but the subdivisions of the target, necessary "touch", and need for concentration (often in a distracting, intoxicating setting) make the game deceptively challenging.

The basic game of darts may award the most points for tosses that penetrate the central bull's eye, with fewer points earned for shots that end up in the concentric circular areas increasingly distant from the center. But the level of complexity can be greatly enhanced by seeking to hit the little 20 wedges of target area that extend from the center to the perimeter of the target. They are not numbered consecutively but must be struck in turn, 1 through 20, in order to win the contest. Dexterity and focus are required to propel the darts precisely where they need to stick.

Foosball

Table football is a casual sport often played in pubs, bars, schools, clubs, and sometimes even the workplace. Players attempt to use solid (plastic, wood, metal, or carbon fiber) little human-like figures mounted on rotating metal bars to kick a ball into the opposing goal. Few rules apply, and the action can get pretty intense, though the International Table Soccer Federation (ITSF) provides guidelines for competition (e.g., high-speed spinning of the rods may be discouraged or illegal). Typical tables measure 2 by 4 feet and employ four bars per side: 2 foosmen on defense, 5 foosmen at midfield, 3 attackmen, and 1 goalkeeper to deflect shots that can reach 56 km/h (35 mph). Two individuals play singles while four players, each controlling two rods, may compete in doubles. There are variations in table size, foosmen size, and team size; for example, a special 7-meter-long table has been created to host 11 players per side. The game is usually just a fun hobby or diversion, though the ITSF regulates play in World Championship and World Cup events.

Horseshoes

Is this an odd use of the uniquely shaped metal objects designed to protect horse's hooves from wear and tear? There are vast supplies of such used footwear, so why not throw them at targets? Actually, the U-shaped horseshoes employed in this game are about twice the size of those that serve as equine hoofwear. Two stakes are placed in the ground (often sand), usually in wood-bound horseshoe "pits" that are 40 feet (12 meters) apart. Players each get two shoes to toss, the first contestant tossing both before her opponent goes. Any part of a shoe must be within 6 inches of the stake, or be a "leaner" on the stake, to earn a point. If the second of the player's shoes is closer to the stake than either of the opponent's shots, two points are earned. A "ringer" gains three points; two ringers get six. But if each player tosses one ringer (or two apiece), they cancel one another and no points are awarded. Games usually run to 21 points; one must win by two.

Lawn Bowling

Toss a little target ball (jack or kitty) some distance and then roll four larger spheres toward it to see who can end up closer to it. It resembles bocce but with less space restriction. What could be simpler? Participants compete on a manicured grass or synthetic bowling green. Of course, you may play on your lawn at home if you like. Task difficulty varies according to the nature of that surface: flat, convex, or uneven. Points or "shots" are awarded for each player's bowls that end up closer to the jack than any of the opponent's bowls. Games usually end at 21 shots.

Marbles

Oh, to be a kid again! The classic child's game of marbles is called "Ringer". Two players "lag" for the right to begin the game; they each toss a marble to see whose ends up closer to a wall ten feet away. Then, in the center of a circle (in the dirt or some other playing surface) ten feet in diameter, they arrange 13 marbles in a crossing pattern (7 x 7 counting the one in the middle twice). The first player "knuckles down" at the perimeter of the circle and launches her "shooter" with the goal of knocking one of the target marbles out of the ring. If that is accomplished, she picks up that marble as her prize and shoots again from wherever her shooter marble came to rest. Knock out seven marbles consecutively and you win! But if she fails to "stick" a marble, her opponent knuckles down at the perimeter of the ring and tries his hand at sticking seven consecutive shots. Better yet, if the other player knocks the opponent's shooter out of the ring, that player claims all of the opponent's marbles and wins the game. If both shooters remain through the entire game, the winner is the one who knocks the most of the 13 marbles out of the ring. Child's play? Gee, it sounds challenging! Variations of the game, both outdoor and indoor versions, offer differing difficulties.

Quoits

Quoits? I've never heard of it. But ring toss? Ah, that sounds familiar. The gentile versions of this game entail efforts to toss rope or plastic rings to encircle wooden stakes or pins; those are garden, deck, pub, fairground, or indoor quoits. But players of the traditional game of quoits in the United Kingdom throw much more substantial steel rings, 5.5 inches in diameter and weighing 5.5 pounds apiece, at a steel spike (hob, mott, or pin) 11 yards away. Those steel pins protrude 3-4 inches out of the clay pits within which they're embedded. The U.S. version uses 4-pound quoits aimed at pins that are 7 yards away and extend 4 inches above the dirt or clay pit. Hence, quoits resembles the game of horseshoes.

Shuffleboard

This game looks like curling made easy. Players use cues (cue sticks measuring 6' 3" or less in length) to slide six-inch-diameter discs down an alley toward a triangular target zone. An official alley is 6 feet wide and 39 feet long, with 6-foot shooting zones behind the scoring triangles at each end. Smaller alleys and table models exist where space is limited. If your opponent has one disc in good scoring position, you may aim to knock it away and leave your own disc there. Any disc ending in the front apex of the triangle earns 10 points; just past that are slightly larger 8-point zones and then larger 7-point zones. Then there is a narrow area called "10 off", a penalty for sure. It's a game for all ages, including young and old, in resort areas and on cruise ships. It entails little athletic effort. It does, however, require eye-hand coordination and that elusive quality called "touch". A willingness to do your opponent dirty may be advantageous, too.

Snooker

Is playing eight-ball or straight pool too tame a game of billiards? Then consider this cue sport using a typical white cue ball along with 21 snooker balls. The object of this pocket billiards game is to sink the 15 red balls, worth one point apiece, along with the yellow (2 points), green (3), brown (4), blue (5), pink (6), and black (7) balls. What a colorful game!

Tiddlywinks

This little indoor game of finesse, contested on a 3 by 6-foot felt mat, involves surprising levels of strategy and a language all its own. Each player uses a plastic squidger disc to flick the small plastic discs, called winks, into a target pot. The game is often contested in teams of two; one pair of partners play with red and blue winks (six of each color), while the other team uses green and yellow winks. If individuals play one another, each commands two colors. One might expect straightforward technique—i.e., aim for the pot and flick your winks into it. But this game of manual dexterity features strategic and tactical planning of offense and defense. For instance, one might squop, or cover an opponent's wink(s) with one's own; since a covered wink may not be played by its owner, the victim of a squop may recover by playing the wink atop his own. Winks may end up in small piles. By game's end, either when time expires (usually about 25 minutes) or someone has potted out all of her winks, players count up their potted and unsquopped winks to determine the higher score. The most tiddlies wins! More could be said about this intriguing game, but one may assume its complexity based on its terms such as blitz, bomb, boondock, bristol, cracker, crud, gromp, lunch, scrunge, and John Lennon memorial shot (a simultaneous boondock which sends a free and squopped wink onto another's wink). The English Tiddlywinks Association, in conjunction with the North American Tiddlywinks Association, sets the rules and runs the big, often international, tournaments.

Are there additional target games not cited here? Of course there are. Humans have an untiring fascination with, and imagination for, the creation of targets at which to throw, roll, or hit projectiles. Carnival games and backyard fun with Jarts come to mind. People skip stones on watery surfaces, with or without particular end points in sight. What about table games such as air hockey and pinball? Those certainly involve targets and skills such as manual dexterity and quickness; those "crazy flipper fingers" helped make The Who's Tommy a pinball wizard. Modern-day, fast-paced, point-and-shoot video games demand unblinking attention, visual-motor control, and quick reflexes to shoot at virtual targets. Tossing bean bags at holes in wooden ramps makes cornhole a favorite party game. Kicking a hacky sack ball, singly or in groups, keeps you on (and off) your toes.

We'll throw or kick just about anything at whatever target we see. There are countless board and card games with winning objectives, but no targets per se. People love to play games.

CHAPTER 8

The Mental Game

• • •

LET'S TAKE A LOOK AT the important topic that deals with the cerebral side of athletics and games. The integration of cognitive, emotional, motivational, spiritual, and physical factors is integral to success at target games. Where would your body be without your brain? You'd be trying to perform sports in a mindless, unfocused manner. You'd be taking dead aim while dead-headed. The brain directs the nervous system to direct bodily movements.

We've all caught glimpses of the psychological mind sets of pro golfers, Olympic competitors, and other high-profile athletes. Some of us have read books, magazine sections, newspaper articles, and online instruction to improve our mental edge. Television commentators and interviewers have helped us peek into the psyches of champion athletes engrossed in the pressure of competition or explaining their reasons for victory. College courses, graduate school programs, and professional journals are devoted to sport psychology. Much is available for anyone interested in delving into the subject.

What is the gist of our current state of awareness and research about the mental side of performance enhancement? Here is some of what we know:

- Preparation is key. Repetition is a great teacher. Trust your training. Ample practice of task-related skills leads to positive expectancy and the confidence to win. Muscle memory comes from habitual rehearsal of skills properly imagined and executed. Morihei Ueshiba, the founder of Aikido, stated, "Strive to understand the truth of oneness of mind and body by training and developing the fundamentals."
- Practice as you plan to perform. Train hard and you're likely to compete hard. Periodically simulate the conditions of an upcoming contest to make practice even more realistic. Then you'll be prepared for the competitive setting and any potential changes to which you must adapt.
- Routine helps. World-class athletes tend to follow habitual patterns of behaviors leading up to their events. This is not superstitious repetition intended to extend good fortune—although good luck charms have proven helpful to many athletes (via the placebo effect). Usually, it is systematically keeping one's mind on a sequence of behaviors that get one ready to perform. Activities that lead to readiness leave no room for thinking about self-doubts and worrying about outcomes and consequences.
- Many athletes listen to music of some sort, according to personal preference, before competing. Shutting out the world of distraction with headphones may be focusing, inspirational, relaxing, or beneficial in some other manner.

Perhaps lyrics motivate; maybe musical rhythms help us tune into our athletic rhythms.
- VMBR helps. Visual-motor-behavioral rehearsal, whether team-oriented guided imagery or individual self-hypnosis, is mental practice of one's actual performance. Research has shown that imagination of movement actually causes muscles and brain cells to fire in a task-related manner; this increases the probability of successful performance of the real thing.
- The mind leads the body. Try this simple experiment: Stand across the room facing a wall, furniture, or other obstacle. After looking at the obstacle for only a second or two, close your eyes and walk briskly up to that object, stopping just short of it. You can trust that your vision records its objective and guides your muscles just the right amount to do this—and more complex athletic feats—with reasonable ease and accuracy. Whether our eyes or other sensory imagery serve as our guide, our brain uses the information to coordinate our subsequent actions.
- Mantras—repetitive sayings—are often utilized as tools toward spiritual enlightenment. Someone on a spiritual path may meditate with a word or phrase playing over and over again in his head such as "peace", "relax", "oneness", "God is love", etc. In athletics, mantras may also serve a useful purpose. A word or expression might help to remind a competitor of a performance key or to reduce the clutter of thoughts and doubts that might cloud the mind in the midst of a contest. Hence, it can be fruitful for a tennis or baseball player to say "eye on the ball" subvocally. A golfer might want to remind herself to "follow the routine"

or use "process" to refocus before each and every shot. A swimmer may guide his strokes with "long and strong" or "reach and rotate" to maximize pulling power.

* Anxiety is a natural component of any competitive situation. According to Mark Twain, "Courage is resistance to fear, mastery of fear—not absence of fear." Welcome nervous energy as an ally. Butterflies in your belly (a felt sense of the neuropeptides there) show that you care; they reflect motivation to succeed. Whether it's a big game, a huge crowd, a TV audience, a bundle of money at stake, or any pressure situation that you face, embrace it. Bring it on!

* There's no I in TEAM—a trite but true assertion. Cooperative chemistry and unselfish sharing make a winning formula. Among wildlife, some of the most effective hunters are prides of female lions and packs of wolves, teaming together to capture prey for the good of the collective. So should an individual athlete's efforts blend with those of his/her teammates in pursuit of victory. Individual glory is secondary and, sometimes, counter-productive to team success. The aim is synergism: the whole is greater than the sum of its parts.

* Most peak performances are accomplished when an athlete or game player is in a flow state, in the zone. Absorption in the here and now, with a minimum of evaluative self-talk, enables the mind and body to unite forces in just the right way for the task at hand. Forget the score or the current standings until after your event. Focus on only one or two key, performance-oriented thoughts. Finding and staying in the zone is not as difficult or magical as one

might think; it simply means giving one's undivided attention to a task or activity at hand. As the Nike slogan wisely advises, "Just Do It."
- Flow, being in the zone, may also be described as mindfulness. Being consciously aware of the here and now, in any context, is associated with both therapeutic progress and spiritual development in everyday life. Performance of any athletic pursuit, as well as enjoyment of it, is enhanced by absorption in the process with minimal regard to thoughts of the past, future, or outcome. Whenever we are engrossed in an activity or experience—e.g., watching a movie, reading an intriguing book, engaging in conversation, listening intently to music, or playing a game—we have flowed into a state of mindfulness. Mindful meditation in motion helps you keep your head in the game and your mind on the target.
- A flow experience, as defined by Mihaly Csikszentmihalyi (1997), occurs when the degree of difficulty of an activity matches an individual's ability to meet that challenge. Flow experiences are correlated with happiness; the more sense of attainment and competence that one gathers from a series of success experiences on tasks worthy of one's capability, the greater the sense of fulfillment and satisfaction. Too easy a game may cause boredom while too great a challenge can stimulate anxiety. An adept college basketball player might get little joy from competing against a bunch of elementary school students, and feel intimidated by taking on NBA players, but he feels great when he and his team win an NCAA Tournament game. Athletics provide a wonderful avenue for the accumulation of flow

experiences when one competes at or near one's level of competence.
- Relaxed concentration is the optimal state of mind and body; W. Timothy Gallwey is the famous author who rightly drew that conclusion through his astute analyses of tennis, golf, skiing, and other sports. Focus on the process, not the outcome, and let go of any tension not directly related to what's needed at the moment. To help grasp this concept, try tensing every muscle in the body, head to toe, and then run; it's easy to feel and see how taut muscles interfere with one another. So, let go of extraneous tension and trust that the muscle activation and cognitive processing needed to perform will be calibrated automatically and most appropriately with minimal conscious direction. Planning and preparation pay dividends when you relax and let the competitive process flow. Trust your aim and let it fly.
- Aikido master Koichi Tohei: "Like the eye of the typhoon, which is always peaceful, inner calm results in great strength of action."
- Mindfulness meditation, practiced once or twice daily for short periods of time, helps set the tone for anxiety management and optimal concentration. Myriad meditation techniques exist, and most of them simplify one's thinking to an awareness of one's breath flowing naturally in and out. Here-and-now awareness of our senses of vision, hearing, smell, taste, and touch can also be invoked as a means of centering and relaxation. Taking time outside the competitive setting to practice the ability to calm and concentrate the mind, with minimal attention to outside

stimuli or internal distractions (e.g., evaluative judgments or worries), can carry over to the athletic arena.
- Neurofeedback, using electroencephalogram (EEG) recordings of brainwave patterns, and biofeedback, using electrocardiogram (EKG), electromyogram (EMG), galvanic skin response (GSR), finger temperature, or simply pulse readings, can help athletes achieve states of relaxed concentration. When we monitor our biological processes, we tend naturally toward greater calmness, lower tension, yet cognitive alertness. Receiving auditory or visual feedback makes the process more robust.
- Confucius said, "Our greatest glory is not in never falling, but in rising every time we fall." Have a structured compensatory strategy on which to rely during competition, especially when feeling out of the zone and out of kilter. It's comforting to have a Plan B in the event that Plan A misfires.
- True victory is victory over oneself. No one can fully control opponents, teammates, and environmental conditions; we can only influence them via self-regulation of our own behaviors. The Taoist philosopher, Lao Tzu, proclaimed that "Mastering others is strength; mastering yourself is true power."
- "It's not whether you win or lose that counts, it's how you play the game." "Winning isn't everything; it's the only thing." Well, which is it? Do we play to win or merely to compete? Winning almost always feels better than losing; only mitigating circumstances (e.g., luck, prejudice by the officials, emotional ties) might make losing feel more justifiable and/or enjoyable. Yet, in every sporting

contest, one side must lose just as the other wins. Does losing thoroughly negate the value of having played a target game? Certainly not! One cannot taste victory without having an opponent willing to risk losing, so the best mindset is appreciation of one's opponent and the process of playing, win or lose. Besides, it's not healthy psychologically either to feel devastated by defeat or to gloat about winning.

- Satisfaction with one's participation in sports, and happiness in life in general, depend upon balancing pleasure and fun while playing along with a sense of purpose and meaning. We want to blend present enjoyment with future benefit, immediate gratification with long-term values and goals (Ben-Shaler, 2007). The happiest athletes are those who play sports for health, competence, competition, camaraderie, accomplishment, and other such reasons, yet also relish the process of training, conditioning, practicing, interacting, and playing along the way.

Sport psychology is worthy of consideration. As the famous New York Yankee and Baseball Hall of Famer, Yogi Berra, once said: "Baseball is ninety percent mental and the other half is physical." "You can observe a lot just by watching." "You've got to be very careful if you don't know where you're going because you might not get there." If those quotations don't prove the value of the mental side of sports, I can't think what does.

Let's take a sport-by-sport look at mental aspects of performance. Which of the aforementioned psychological principles and practices, and perhaps some additional guidelines, apply directly to the following assortment of target games?

Archery: A seminal volume in the genre of sport psychology and spirituality is *Zen in the Art of Archery* by Eugen Herrigel. Visual acuity and a steady hand are essential; such eye-hand-body coordination is part of still-point focus, an alert meditative state. Self-trust is key. So is distraction control; one must not let any extraneous movement or sound sway one from concentrating on the task/target integration. Conscious regulation of (or unconscious trust in) your breathing promotes a steady aim and smooth release of the bow string. Harvey Penick's golf adage, "Take dead aim", applies fully as you look to the center of the bull's eye, not merely that vicinity.

Mr. Herrigel's immersion into archery was not a smooth and easy journey. He had to think, analyze, work, and practice very hard to understand the mental and physical components of improvement. Persistence did, however, pay off with progress. Gilbert Arland adds the following: "When an archer misses the mark, he turns and looks for the fault within himself. Failure to hit the bull's eye is never the fault of the target. To improve your aim—improve yourself."

Baseball: Attentional control is key. Outfielders and infielders must stay alert to baserunners, where to throw, the number of outs, signals from coaches, and other situational cues. Visual attention is most directly important—keep your eye on the ball when batting and catching. There are multiple targets involved:

The pitcher aims the ball at home plate, the batter strives to hit the ball to a particular location, fielders track and catch the ball, then throw to teammates who may need to tag the runner who perceives the next base as his proximal target.

Baseball players need sufficient frustration tolerance to cope calmly with umpires' calls (safe/out, ball/strike, fair/foul, right or wrong), errors by teammates, crowd taunts, base-running mistakes, etc. Relaxed concentration is conducive to better bat speed and timing, fielders' reaction times, and running speed; relax, trust, and follow your eyes. Shrewd strategy plays a huge role—e.g., when to bunt, steal, change a pitcher, give up an intentional walk. Baseball decisions are far from straightforward; snap judgments and risk-taking are parts of the game: "Progress always involves risk; you can't steal second base and keep your foot on first" (Frederick Wilcox). Cooperation is key, with no room for jealousy in this team game played with individual components (e.g., pitcher and catcher must be on the same wavelength). Players need mentally to adapt to wind, sun, shadows, heat, cold, and other environmental factors. Pitch, hit, run, throw—there's a lot more to baseball than those basic skills.

Ken Ravizza, a psychological consultant to major league baseball teams, applied "The Six Rs" to the sport: Ready, Respond, Recognize, Release, Regroup, and Refocus. A pitcher, for instance, must read the signs from his catcher, agree to one, and prepare to make his pitch in that intended manner. He responds with a pitch toward the catcher's mitt, with the appropriate delivery (speed and spin). He recognizes the result—a strike, ball, foul, hit, or home run. If that outcome is negative, the pitcher may mutter a curse word, walk off the mound, or otherwise release his negative emotional reaction. It's then time to regroup; perhaps the catcher, infielders, and pitching coach confer on the mound. The pitcher sighs and gathers himself to continue. He refocuses, thinking briefly about his standard routine and trusting that he's ready to pitch again. This systematic cycle of coping with adversity may be useful for other baseball positions as well as for athletes in any sport who need to release frustration before regaining self-control and resuming his/her best effort.

Basketball: Preparation (e.g., set offensive plays, defensive assignments, shooting skill) blends with spontaneity (e.g., switch defense, look for an open teammate, help defensively, rebound, dive for a loose ball, take off on a fast break, go with the flow). Players must be confident, not cocky, and fully unselfish. Vision and visualization help—e.g., see a shot entering the center of the hoop (e.g., free throw), where a bank shot should meet the backboard, the direction and distance of a rebound based on a shot in flight, where and when to pass to a moving teammate. Stay loose and relaxed, letting muscles activate themselves just the right amount as needed to move one's body and the ball. "Touch" is best in a state of relaxed concentration. So is attention to coaches, team members, and situations. Since human perception, judgment, and sometimes error play huge roles in basketball—i.e., the calls by the officials—players need to tolerate the frustration of fouls wrongly called, fouls missed or ignored by officials, and other erroneous calls (out of bounds, traveling, three seconds, goaltending). Self-restraint is needed to cope with officials' calls, right or wrong, as well as hostile fans, provocation by an opponent, or the need to refrain from fouling out of a game. It's good for basketball players to have an inner clock, sensitivity to time, in order to shoot just before the shot clock expires or a period ends.

In basketball, as in any fast-moving sport, the Eastern concept of *mu-shin* comes into play. This means no-mind or empty mind. That is not to say empty-headedness, but rather open-mindedness. *Mu-shin* is a state without inhibiting expectation, guided not by assumption of what might happen next but instead ready to respond instantaneously to whatever event or situation might actually be taking shape. Unencumbered by prediction, the present and open mind reacts to unforeseeable occurrences in the most efficient and effective way possible. For example, if a player moves as if to shoot, a defender may launch herself in that direction to block the shot only to see the apparent shooter instead rifle a pass to her teammate or dribble drive to the basket. Shooting hoops is a delightful and complex blend of mind and body.

Biathlon: This creative, taxing sport embodies the reconciliation of yin and yang—settling down for precise fine motor movements in the wake of strenuous gross motor exertion. Cross-country ski racing is a high-energy exercise that stimulates the sympathetic nervous system which, in turn, triggers rapid breathing and heart rates, large-muscle activation, and growing fatigue. Skiers must have proper form, pacing, and stamina to endure the strenuous portions of their two-pronged event. Arriving at a shooting site, they need a reliable strategy to calm, restore, and center themselves for accurate target shooting. Conscious breath control is an obvious need. Purposeful sighs—forceful exhalations—can quickly restore equilibrium. So can awareness of one-point (mentally focusing on the center of the body) and shrugging of shoulders. Time is of the essence during both phases of this sport, so one must blend efficiency with accuracy while shooting. Marksmen lightly squeeze the trigger when certain of their shot. They must concentrate solely on their own performance, not those of fellow competitors or the reactions of officials and any gallery that may be watching. While skiing, however, one must be acutely aware of other competitors in order to pass, draft, avoid collision, and jostle for position. If a biathlete must also adapt to weather conditions such as cold (chilled fingers), snow (or sleet or rain), or wind (affecting bullet flight), the sport becomes that much more taxing from a physical and mental standpoint. The esoteric sport of chess boxing must demand similarly rapid transition and adjustment back-and-forth between physiological activation and calm centering.

Bowling: The central tenets and practices of sport psychology apply directly to bowling. Centered relaxation enables a bowler to maintain balance from start to finish of the throwing motion of the dense, heavy ball; you must trust your muscles (feet, legs, hips, back, shoulders, arm, wrist, hand, and fingers) to activate in just the right sequence and intensity. Visualization of the shot prepares you for execution. See the path of the ball from its release point (the foul line) to the pins, then let the throw unfold and happen naturally. You must reconcile two targets, near and far, small and big; a great bowler picks a spot, a particular board, on which to set the ball at the top of the lane, and simultaneously maintains awareness of the distant pocket in the constellation of pins. Never get discouraged and feel tempted to give up when behind. Stay optimistic. A string of strikes, when an opponent has an open frame, can quickly close any scoring gap. Conversely, stay level-headed and focused when ahead in a match because a costly split can be only one throw away. In big tournaments and small, an audience can be a distraction. Shut out their influence. Bowling is a graceful art that requires composure more than getting charged up.

Curling: This Scottish/Canadian classic needs analysis, planning, strategy, and flexibility because it is an interdependent sport. The stone is tossed, then its distance and direction are influenced by the actions of two teammates. Players must synchronize their planning and execution, with real-time alterations possible as each shot unfolds. And unlike bowling, where each competitor's action is discrete, curling circumstances change due to its alternating-shot format at the same target. You must be ready to go with the flow, adapting fluidly to the situation set up by the other team's shots and the current score. The person who launches the stone, by virtue of its heavy weight, must be centered and relaxed. Visualize its path in order to apply optimal "touch" and curl at the point of release. The sweepers must be flexible, able to see ahead (actually to their sides) how the toss is unfolding and heeding the advice of their other teammates so they can steer, correct, adjust, and pinpoint accordingly. Similar to a game of chess, players should strive to anticipate the next, next, and next moves by the opposing team as well as their own game plan—yet perceive the reality with fresh eyes after every turn.

Darts: Eye-hand-body coordination is key, so relaxed and centered is the way to be. Maintain a light touch. While a bowler or golfer may want to envision the path of the ball all the way from the player to its objective, a dart thrower should focus purely on the specific point in the target ahead (because of the short distance covered). You must adapt to different games, different targets—e.g., slivers of the board vs. the bull's eye. If you happen to engage in competition in a traditional pub setting, expect a decline in performance in direct proportion to the quantity of adult beverage consumed.

Football: One's level of relaxed concentration, or body/mind activation, varies considerably by position. The quarterback, for instance, strives to embody poise, calm centeredness, and keen alertness to the complete picture on the field. Linemen, both offensive and defensive, have specific duties to bear in mind on each play, but they better have their muscles taut and ready to explode at the snap of the ball. Picture a great middle linebacker (e.g., Dick Butkus, Ray Nitschke, Mike Singletary, Lawrence Taylor) and you'll likely see intensity, raw energy, and coiled power, more than calm composure, awaiting the start of the play. Wide receivers and defensive backs need to be cool and collected, yet ready to run like the wind. Running backs may resemble linebackers, alert to their assignments but ready to collide with force.

Like basketball, football calls for the harmony of preparation and spontaneity. Members of a team must learn and be prepared to execute their individual actions/roles for any given play, yet be ready to ad lib. Examples: (1) The QB drops back to pass but sees his receivers covered, so he either runs forward, or rolls out of the pocket and throws the ball out of bounds; (2) An OL aims to block a DL or LB who's no longer there, so he adjusts quickly and blocks someone else; (3) A blitz prompts the need to block the extra invading players; (4) A RB heads for a designated "hole" that suddenly closes, so he bounces or spins to one side or another; (5) Defensive players execute their role or cover their zone, but keep their eyes open for what is truly happening and attack the QB, RB, WR, or potential receiver as indicated. The best QBs "see" a pass completion before it actually happens, maybe before releasing the ball; visualization enables the QB to "lead" his receiver or throw to a spot before his battery mate even turns in that direction. Vision and anticipation empower a DB to read the eyes of a QB, anticipate a pass, and move into position to break up or intercept it; similarly, a DL or LB might shoot a gap and make a tackle in the backfield. Players must focus their attention on coaches, the QB, sideline signals, checks at the line of scrimmage, etc. Woe to the player who listens poorly or forgets easily, breaking the huddle and forgetting the play at hand. An individual's blunder can be his team's undoing. As Doug Whaley, former GM of the Buffalo Bills, once said, "Playing football no doubt is very physically, mentally, and emotionally challenging, and that's all part of what makes the game so compelling to play and watch."

Golf: The golfers we most admire tend to display steely resolve (e.g., Tiger Woods, Jack Nicklaus), easygoing panache (e.g., Fred Couples, Fuzzy Zeller), or a flair for the dramatic (e.g., Chi Chi Rodriguez, Lee Trevino). Easy smiles, self-deprecating grins, and apparent imperturbability seem intimately related to success on the links. Winning pros seem neither distressed by bad nor elated by good shots. They tend to play in a steady state, with low-key or short-term displays of emotion. Indeed, relaxed concentration enables them to keep their grip light and flexible, their touch optimal, and their muscles activated just the right amount from the energetic tee shot through the relatively inert putt. They use visualization explicitly; most serious modern players (e.g., Jordan Speith, Jason Day, Rory McIlroy, Rickie Fowler) stand behind their ball and picture the ideal shot before moving into position beside the ball and seeing that target in their mind's eye from that perspective. Since "obstacles are those frightful things you see when you take your eyes off your goals" (anonymous), good golfers look not at water hazards and clumps of thick bushes but rather at ideal landing zones. Imagery often extends to <u>feeling</u> the proper swing, as well.

Golfers must be fully present. The process of executing each shot determines, and hence outweighs, its outcome. Focus on each individual stroke and the scorecard will take care of itself. Thus, since golf is such a balanced coordination of mental and physical energies, there is a premium placed on distraction control. Potential influences of spectators, playing partners, noises, attempts at gamesmanship, and inner thoughts between shots (money, glory, home, family, etc.) must be stifled or sent on their way. Touring pros may excel at this with apparent ease; but the task is maddeningly difficult for most mere mortals on the links.

<u>Hockey</u>: As in basketball, hockey players must maintain mental awareness of the locations of their teammates, both present and imminent. Crisp passing, shooting, and defending depend on such mental, visual, and auditory acuity. The speed of the game demands quick decisions, reflexes, and fluidity. Skaters need simultaneously to enjoy states of relaxed concentration and intense muscle activation. Relaxation aids reflex, high-speed actions and reactions. The fast-paced game, with collisions galore,

requires frequent rest (line changes) to enable out-of-breath players to recover their second, third, etc., wind. There is not time to "skate"—that is, to let one's mind drift. One must go all-out, knowing that periods of rest will soon follow. Broad peripheral vision of the ice is critical to enable spur-of-the-moment actions. And toughness is a prerequisite, as it is in football and many other sports. Hockey players must be willing to bump, collide, and even fight for control of the puck.

Lacrosse: This is a true contact sport. Players must be prepared mentally and physically to give as well as to receive. Those engaged in the face-off process must be particularly pugnacious. They need strategies and adaptability to gain possession of the ball. Naturally, the entire team has much to learn and execute strategically. Positional differences are robust. Attackmen must be active yet patient, opportunistic and unselfish. Long-stick defenders need aggressive tenacity to stay on their assigned players (or zones) but the flexibility to shift assignments (switch off) or to attack the opposing players when a rush allows. Mid-fielders strive to balance offensive and defensive skills with physical speed and mental agility. The goalie must be centered and courageous, ready with fast reflexes that are best enabled by a state of relaxed concentration (i.e., calm readiness). All players need the mentality to go all-out, to leave nothing on the field, since ample teammates and flowing substitutions are available to spell anyone who grows winded.

Martial Arts: *Mu-shin* ("empty mind") applies directly and strongly to any and all fighting arts. Don't let expectation encumber you; be open-minded and prepared for anything. If a boxer expects and plans for a left hook to the head, his opponent may surprisingly land a right punch to the torso. In wrestling or judo, one must feel the opponent's moves spontaneously rather than anticipate them and apply inappropriate counter-attacks. The stakes are high. A delayed defensive tactic can leave you lying on the mat, injured. There is no room or time for extraneous thought. Self-defense requires flow, fully present sensory perception and action potential. The fighting arts also require *chudo*, the middle path of assertiveness that lies between passivity (playing the victim) and aggression (attacking recklessly and hurtfully).

Soccer: As in lacrosse, basketball, football, and assorted other sports, positional differences matter a lot. Those who play forward/striker need an aggressive, type-A personality. Midfielders may be more analytical, more global because all play goes through them. They must let the game come to them, cognizant and perceptive of how plays are developing and unfolding. Defensive players must be pugnacious, ready to sacrifice their bodies to stop attacks at all costs. The goalie, naturally, needs constant vigilance. There is no daydreaming allowed! Intermittently, the goalie must be on high alert as the ball approaches, yet remain relaxed enough to stay centered and not commit too soon to a shot. The goalie in soccer, as in hockey, lacrosse, water polo, and similar sports, needs to spring fully into action at a split-second's notice. A soccer player must blend the ability to stay within her role/zone with the skill to improvise and react to opportunity. One's mentality should be tireless, enduring, ready to run until she drops. You must be self-possessed enough to avoid handballs, minimize fouls, and channel frustration and anger into constructive energy expenditure.

Swimming: As stated, it is debatable whether or not swimming is in any way a target sport. But proper form may be considered a worthy point of concentration and emphasis, as may one's split times in a long race. Furthermore, swimmers may track their competitors in nearby lanes, hanging back to draft off their wakes to save energy to pass them with finishing kicks. When swimmers get nervous or tired, their strokes tend to shorten and slow their progress. So, the optimal mind set is, not surprisingly, one of flow: accept mild anxiety as a source of energy, stay relatively relaxed, be mindful of proper technique, let the race unfold at a swift but natural pace, periodically focus on full breath exhalations and inhalations, and trust the process to determine progress and outcome.

Tennis: Mental factors that apply especially to tennis probably suit themselves to other racquet sports, as well. The optimal level of cognitive, emotional, and physical activation is something between that needed for best golf and football—calm yet dynamic, muscles ready yet without tension of unnecessary muscular contractions that tend to interfere with reflexive reactivity and smooth movement. Pauses between points are opportunities for releasing tension, refocusing, and readying oneself for the next serve. Tennis demands a dynamic blend of power and range of motion.

Since mind and body are so intricately integrated with one another, performance enhancement depends not only on training for one's sport and honing one's mental approach to the game. Vision also plays a critical role in each and every one of the sports and games cited herein. Many individuals and teams engage in sport-specific vision training. For instance, basketball players need to shift their gaze fluidly among both friendly and opposing players in order to know how to react, both offensively and defensively; then they need to devote full focus to the inside of the basket or a spot on the backboard as they launch shots. Split-second shifts in visual attention can be improved with drills and practice. Wider visual fields (i.e., peripheral vision) can be cultivated through vision therapy. Visual acuity helps with centering and balance. Every sort of athlete needs to be able to see the ball and their various targets with clarity and efficiency.

Sports medicine is another domain worthy of mention (though not in considerable detail here). Physicians, physicians' assistants, nurses, and athletic trainers help players to optimize their health, recover from injuries, and train proper mechanics so that body parts work in coordinated fashion. So do physical therapists and chiropractors. Pain management is a crucial facet of sport psychology. Sports nutritionists help at the training table, fortifying athletes with the nutrients they need for proper mood, focus, and physicality. Modern-day athletes often employ a team of consultants to enhance aspects of physical and mental performance of their various endeavors.

CHAPTER 9

Additional Factors

• • •

In every one of the sports discussed herein, varied sets of skills are needed to perform with confidence and competence. Training and practice, learning and experience, physical and mental skills, all pay dividends. But there are external elements to many sports that add to their levels of difficulty. Some factors well beyond the control of athletes influence the outcomes of their contests. Here are some of those factors, in no particular order, and the roles they play.

Luck

Sometimes a golf shot is right on line, hit the perfect distance, but lands atop a tiny section of uneven ground and bounds off-course. Other times, of course, an off-target shot gets a favorable bounce that propels it toward the hole. And when you hit into a tree, strike a spectator, or encounter a gust of wind, there's no telling whether its effect will be beneficial or harmful. "That's the way the ball bounces" is an expression that applies not only to golf, but also to football and other sports. The pigskin, by virtue of its oblong shape, can go any which way when punted, fumbled, or deflected—sometimes landing in the hands of an offensive player for a gain or a score, or sometimes in the possession of a defender heading the other direction. A soccer goalie can make a great save, only to have the ball bounce off one of his teammates and into the goal. Deflections off other unsuspecting players score goals in hockey, too. In any sport or game, you may have your "personal best" performance but, by bad luck, lose to a competitor who likewise soared past personal expectation. It's your lucky day—or it's not.

Officiating

Games such as billiards and darts, or sports such as archery and marksmanship, have fairly straightforward targets and scores. Whoever throws a javelin, discus, or shot the farthest, without committing a foot foul, emerges victorious from a track and field competition. Violations are possible but uncommon in sports such as swimming and running—the fastest time wins. But many pastimes, including our most popular spectator sports, are powerfully influenced by the perceptions and judgments of non-participants.

In baseball, it is the home plate umpire who decides if a pitch is call strike three or ball four, if a runner is safe or out at home plate. Is a hit fair or foul? Did a runner evade a tag at second or third, beat a throw to first base, stay in the base path? It's the officials, not the players, who determine when a fumble occurs, a reception is made or bobbled, a catch is made inbounds or not, and whether or not the ball has broken the plane of the goal line on the football field. Penalties are called and assessed numerous times every game. Football players, besides those directly making a tackle, have their hands on one another every play;

when is a holding penalty called, ignored, or left unseen? People in striped shirts roam the playing fields of soccer, lacrosse, and rugby, jog up and down the basketball court, monitor any shenanigans occurring in a water polo match, and regulate play in volleyball. Might "touch fouls" be called more often against the visiting but not the home team in basketball? Tournament tennis is marked by the presence of lines people strategically placed on the court, with a chair umpire in place to voice decisive and critically important judgments. (The technology of "cyclops" has taken most of the guesswork out of tennis calls of in or out.) Golfers take pride in their integrity, independently enforcing the rules and code of ethics on a routine basis; but there's a batch of officials at every professional tournament, as well, there to aid judgments and ensure compliance. Winners of diving, skating, gymnastics, martial arts, and various competitions are determined by the perceptions and scoring by judges as much as by one's actual performance. Do officials make mistakes? Are biases possible? Might their subjective rulings determine the outcome of a contest? Do they help keep contests fair and square? Yes, yes, yes, and yes.

Weather

Oy, the whims of weather. Mother Nature may play a role in any outdoor sport. Wind affects the direction, trajectory, and carry of baseballs, golf balls, and footballs. It may even alter the accuracy of a swiftly moving arrow or bullet. Rain or snow makes a football slippery. So do cold hands. When agile changes of direction are needed on a football, soccer, or lacrosse playing field, wet grass and mud can wreak havoc with footing. Tennis matches get postponed when water begins to gather on the court, making traction slip away. Rain can make a golf grip slip. But it can make a golf green grip. It can be extra challenging to catch a high fly ball, or a punt, when you look up and get blinded by the sun. Thomas S. Monson reminds us: "We cannot direct the wind; but we can adjust the sails."

Injuries

How often and seriously players get hurt may be an indirect measure of how challenging their sport may be. Given the violent collisions intrinsic to the sports, football and hockey quickly come to mind; back-up players must be ready to be substituted into games on short notice. Boxers beat up each other; so, perhaps, do various other martial artists while wrestlers tangle in ways that twist, torque, and strain every muscle in one another's bodies. Rugby and lacrosse can be rough-and-tumble sports. But even less overtly aggressive sports entail intense, strenuous action that can injure participants. It is not at all uncommon for baseball players, no matter what positions they play, to move on and off the disabled list. Soccer players hobble one another during their battles for control of the ball. Tennis players cramp or suffer from foot, ankle, leg, back, and shoulder injuries. Ski and snowboard racers sometimes endure hellacious, high-speed falls. Even golfers, who appear to do little more than stroll through manicured parks that resemble Zen gardens, undergo medical treatment for their backs, wrists, and shoulders. Ice packs abound after basketball games, swimming meets, track & field events, etc. Risk of injury is surely a measure of courage and determination, if not task difficulty, when we ponder assorted sports.

Technological Development

Is it more or less challenging to hit a long, straight golf shot now than it was a generation ago? Given the improvements in equipment and training that have occurred over time, it appears that the game has become easier. Shafts are stronger yet more flexible than ever; clubheads are designed to be more forgiving of mis-hits as well as more streamlined and aerodynamic. Balls have been engineered to fly farther than ever before. Putters come in every shape, size, length, weight, and composition, the better to nudge the ball toward the hole. Golf-specific exercise regimens are the rule of the day, helping players to develop more clubhead speed. It's no wonder that so many classic golf courses have been lengthened and re-designed, and newer courses built longer than ever before, to accommodate the advances that have occurred. If you play competitive golf and fail to take advantage of the latest technologies, you may face a severe disadvantage versus your opponents.

Have other sports similarly evolved, reducing levels of difficulty and/or providing competitive edges? Frisbees are no more round than in the past, but their precise weights and designs make them fly better for disc golf and ultimate frisbee contests. Football remains an injury-riddled sport due to training regimens that make players bigger, stronger, faster, and more hazardous on contact; their uniforms have evolved to provide more protection, but safety remains a major issue. Concussions and the chronic traumatic encephalopathy (CTE) they potentially cause are increasingly in the news, and there may not be sufficient technology (e.g., in helmet design) to make football and other contact sports safe. Collisions in hockey similarly offset equipment improvements with players who pack more of a wallop. The design and composition of skis have changed myriad times over the years; racers want the latest technology to shave thousandths of seconds off their times. In myriad sports and games, technical enhancements of training and equipment matter.

Audience Effects

How hard is it to make a basketball free throw in the din of an arena, with thousands of opposing fans yelling and waving in an effort to distract you? How hard is it to make a putt in absolute silence, with no movement visible within your field of vision? How much easier does an athletic performance become with a crowd of supporters rooting for you? Psychologists have studied audience effects. One simple example is running: When someone is jogging along a road, and either a pedestrian or vehicle approaches, the runner tends to speed up his/her pace. We all feel a natural drive to perform, to impress onlookers. Supportive fans likely enhance performance even more. An adversarial crowd of fans, on the other hand, can "steal your ki", take you out of your rhythm, and help turn the tide in favor of their hometown hero(es).

Personal Distractions

Is an athlete on the verge of her/his first big victory feeling stress attendant to that prospect? Does added pressure come from prize money, competing for one's national (or state, college, high school) team, or playing for the honor of a recently deceased loved one? Are you still rehabbing from a worrisome injury? Might you have relationship issues on your mind? Are you competing in a novel place, unfamiliar conditions, or other circumstances that may undermine concentration? Does an undisclosed ailment or subtle pain weigh heavily on your mind? Perhaps the visage of a strikingly attractive person intrudes on your mental focus. Did last night's dinner fortify you with energy and stamina, or leave you with indigestion or even a touch of food poisoning? Do insects bug you?

Idiosyncratic events may affect one's mindset as well as the mechanics of one's performance. Do such distractions influence one sport more than another? Maybe individual sports such as golf or tennis, dependent on self-reliance, are thrown more out of whack than team sports where one's mates might successfully compensate for minor letdowns by individuals. But it could be the other way around: one distracted mis-play could throw off team timing, rhythm, and chemistry, resulting in a poor outcome.

Altered States of Consciousness

Alcohol, drugs, and athletics don't mix—at least not well. As engrossing and exhilarating as engagement in sports and games can be, there is still ample spare time for athletes to feel tempted to alter their states of mind—a natural drive according to Dr. Andrew Weil (1973) and numerous psychologists. Happiness is predicated upon a blend of the familiar (sameness, homeostasis, comfort zone, normal state of mind) and variety (changing perception with the aid of travel, movies, music, reading, and/or mind-altering substances). Drinking beer, wine, or liquor can be a pleasant, stress-relieving diversion. As a central nervous system (CNS) depressant, however, alcohol follows its disinhibiting effects with suppression of thinking, mood, and coordination. Fatigue left over from alcohol consumption can impair athletic performance to some degree for 24-72 hours. Performance-enhancing drugs (PEDs) may assist healing and performance as advertised, but not without side effects and potential disqualification. Prescription drugs may be medically justified and helpful, but perhaps with side effects deleterious to athletic activity. Recreational drugs, besides being illegal, may bring about refreshing changes in consciousness, may augment or interfere with performance, and, again, could cause adverse reactions and fatigue. All-natural approaches to athletics and target games bring healthy bodies, clear minds, and guilt-free consciences to competitive arenas.

Scruples

What if your moral fiber prohibits you from hitting an opponent hard in a football or hockey game? Injuring someone, even in the heat of athletic battle, would wound your conscience. Perhaps your sense of good sportsmanship causes you to ease up and let down your guard when you have a substantial lead in a contest, thereby enabling your opponent to launch a furious comeback. An opposing player may have a severely underdeveloped sense of morality, prompting him or her to deliver a crippling blindside blow to you or one of your teammates. Dirty plays may be penalized, but not before they injure an opponent and knock him out of the game.

The Golden Rule sometimes takes a backseat to acts of gamesmanship. A famed pro football team has allegedly bent the rules a few times to increase their chances of winning. Casual golfers have been known to forget to count a stroke here and there or, conversely, to "sandbag" for a higher handicap and better chance of winning an upcoming match or tournament. Rules of etiquette get breached to disturb and distract an opponent. Taunting, arguing, and other such unsportsmanlike behaviors pop up now and then. Levels of moral development can play significant roles in how target games are conducted.

Spiritual Issues

No, I'm not referring to divine intervention. I find it hard to believe that The Almighty chooses to take sides, and intervene actively, in sporting events; chances are good that both teams include people of faith. Furthermore, I'm an empiricist who has never seen proof of any such influence, no matter the claims of righteous combatants. But one's spiritual beliefs can play a role in how one plays the game. This factor ties in with the previous one: competitors on a path toward spiritual well-being might grapple with matters of sportsmanship and the value of doing the right thing, even at the expense of athletic intensity. Those without any spiritual leanings might seek unfair advantages without a thought about athletic integrity. Sports that rely upon close interaction of opposing players—e.g., basketball, football, or lacrosse vs. swimming, tennis, or bowling—may be most strongly affected, for better or worse, by such matters.

Spiritual development may be enriched by prayer or meditation, the reading of religious or spiritual materials, and the act of embracing one's faith. Any and all of those activities can enhance self-confidence, determination, perseverance, stress management, and ability to focus during competition.

CHAPTER 10

Discussion

• • •

Which sport tires you 'til you feel lame?
   Which victory deserves true fame?
   Which athlete can make the claim
   That his sport's not the least bit tame?
   What's the hardest sport or game?

So, which of the major or minor sports entails the most difficulty?

"America's Game" is baseball, partly due to its native origin and popularity, but also due to its challenges. Pitches may be spinning toward a batter at speeds up to 100 miles per hour—just a blur to a batter with keen eyesight and concentration. Maybe the ball is approaching slightly more slowly but is curving, sinking, arcing, or perhaps threatening his physical well-being by coming straight at him. The player tries to strike the immediate target, the ball, with a "meaty" part of the tubular bat in order to propel it with speed and accuracy toward the secondary target, either over the fence or into a gap between players in the field who are madly striving to catch the sphere and spoil the batter's effort. This must be accomplished under team and fan pressure to succeed and, in a typical setting, under the influence of crowd noise, verbal taunting, and a wealth of visual and auditory distractions. And what about the role of the pitcher? As we know, he tries to be the master multi-tasker. His catcher is specifying the target, more or less, by holding out his mitt for a second or two, and it can be darn hard to place the ball in that target zone pitch after pitch, inning after inning. Fielders sprint in whatever direction is needed to retrieve a batted ball, sometimes risking injury as they lay out or leap up to make a catch. Runners need speed and, often, the skill of sliding into a base. Neither pitching, hitting, fielding, nor base-running is easy business. Professional baseball may first come to mind, but softball, youth baseball, and all levels of the game offer similar challenges.

Perhaps basketball offers less difficult circumstances. After all, the player can shoot it with his/her hands, without need to wield an implement. The ball never travels at blazing speed, as it does in many of the sports described in this book. The game is usually played indoors, in comfortable temperature, with the assistance of teammates. Of course, there are people swatting at the ball, trying to steal it from you or block your shot. The 9-inch ball must fit into the 18-inch hoop, tossed from distances typically ranging from one to twenty-five feet. With defenders rushing toward you, a shot clock winding down, and fans screaming for or against you, you often have only a split-second to launch any given shot. If you'd like to ramp up the difficulty of regular basketball, try playing the game riding on the backs of donkeys or balanced atop unicycles. Donkey basketball is a fairly common spectator sport with fund-raising—and fun-raising—in mind. Unicycle basketball has risen to the level of having an annual world championship tournament.

Football is at the top of the American heap of popularity in spite of, and because of, the hazards endemic to the sport. One false step can cripple a player's ankle or knee; one collision can cause concussive brain trauma. The complex strategies and teamwork...the speed and ferocity...the grace and power...the geometry... If you want to consider big instead of small goals, the end zone of a football field is relatively enormous—10 yards deep and 53 1/3 yards wide (and even larger in Canadian Football)—so maybe it's an easy target to hit. Teams have multiple ways by which to score points. One large challenge is that the quarterback must throw an odd-shaped ball to a moving target while large people with a license to hit converge on both him and his potential receiver. Fortunately, the QB and his receivers, under the guidance of their coaches, are collaborating to converge on a path to the goal. But their adversaries likewise use teamwork to try to block advancement toward that target. If airborne routes to score seem precarious, then feel free to run with the ball to the end zone; of course, you still have fast, muscular guys chasing and trying to tackle you along the way. It sounds easy to move the ball ten yards every three or four plays to keep possession of the ball and make progress—but the statistics prove it's not so easy. Then what could be difficult about placekicking the odd-shaped football through the 18 ½-foot-wide uprights 40 or 50 yards away amid raucous fan noise and mind-numbing pressure to succeed? Plenty.

Football (soccer) is #1 in worldwide popularity despite, and due to, the paucity of scoring. Fancy footwork, near misses, and great saves cause waves of cheering among a team's supporters. Actual scores cause paroxysms of pleasure. Given that the game requires so little equipment, millions of people of all cultures, ages, and socio-economic levels can play; they learn to appreciate the skills and stamina of accomplished players. The best players need to be able to run far and fast, and to be well-coordinated, so they deservedly become international stars.

Golf offers complex challenges. The average golfer knows that pro players, male and female, are really, really good. The pros make look easy what is actually a taxing, complicated series of mind-body tasks. Club and shot selection may be ambiguous and tricky. Clubhead speed must be generated as one swings on balance, winding up and releasing with minimal lateral movement, in order to achieve accuracy. Even though etiquette dictates that distractions by spectators and playing partners be minimized, it can be nerve-wracking to have varied numbers of observers (from one player to tens of thousands of fans and millions of TV viewers) witnessing your every move and utterance. Golf course hazards and adverse weather conditions invite wayward shots. It's remarkable that the 1% of good players navigate from tee to hole in 2-5 shots while the other 99% of us may need many more swipes at the ball to guide it into its target.

Hockey requires much more than the ability to shoot the puck at a relatively small, guarded target using a stick to propel (or deflect, redirect, or block) the shot. Players must also be expert ice skaters! Streaking over ice at high speed, they must be able to slow, stop, change direction, accelerate, spin, skate backwards, and integrate their movements with those of their teammates and opponents. Free-flowing hockey teams resemble a skilled group of dancers, or a troupe of jugglers passing clubs, though with less structure. Set plays are planned and practiced, but much passing and playing happen on the fly. Body contact may be regulated by some rules, but on-ice collisions are surely not trivial.

How, given the attributes and complexities of athletic endeavors, do we decide which sports most intrigue and challenge us? Human beings are largely dichotomous thinkers by nature. Life is good or bad, happy or sad. Political races generally come down to a two-party system. We give thumbs-up or thumbs-down. In addition to polarized thinking, people are prone to superlatives, estimating which entity is the best, hardest, etc. So, can we arrive at an opinion about which target sport is the most difficult?

One criterion by which to compare athletic endeavors is how hard they are to win. Another is to consider the level of skill needed to play the sport at highly competitive, or even basic, levels. A third approach is to examine the sports' participants themselves, comparing them in terms of their all-around athletic physique and prowess.

Winning & Losing

People are clearly competitive by nature. That can be a healthy drive or an unhealthy preoccupation. We can use sports for motivation to become fit, master skills, conquer fears, manage anxiety, cope with losing, and be a gracious winner. We always, without exception, prefer winning to losing. And the discrepancy between victory and defeat is distinct; very few contests end in a draw. Defeat, after all, feels frustrating, maddening, and saddening. We analyze losses in "shoulda/coulda/woulda" terms, often pointing fingers of blame at various specifics. Coaches get fired and players get traded. Winning, on the other hand, brings satisfaction, glory, and a felt sense of triumph over adversity. More lucrative professional contracts follow. The enjoyment of victory totally out-trumps the disappointment of defeat; the consequences of sporting outcomes may help us gauge just how important and difficult an event might be.

Since all target games—indeed all sports—have winners and losers, it's hard to compare such pursuits on the criterion of win-loss percentage. Reality says that winners and losers are interdependent; we cannot have one without the other. Losers are valuably indispensable! Besides, it could be contrary to one's sense of self-worth and well-being to put much stock into the difference between the two. Habitual winners may risk going beyond self-confidence to states of self-righteousness and a sense of moral superiority; chronic losers can suffer demoralization and a dispiriting loss of self-esteem. Perhaps the intensity of the joy of victory and the agony of defeat is a measure of a sport's quality. Let's appreciate <u>both</u> sides of every sporting outcome. There can be no contest without the risk of victory vs. defeat. Besides, just as people can learn from their mistakes in everyday life, athletic losers can gain motivation to get better until they become winners.

How else does the win-lose proposition factor into our weighing of a sport's relative complexity and difficulty? Are the hardest sports the ones most difficult to win? Is it harder to win—by doing more training, devising better strategies, and exerting more effort—than to lose? Perhaps recovery from defeat—getting over it emotionally, learning from the setback, and improving one's game as a result—is a measure of athletic difficulty. Does a pattern of winning imply that a game is relatively easy? Just because the NY Yankees used to win the World Series in bunches does not mean that baseball is an elementary game. Neither do multiple victories by Sam Snead, Jack Nicklaus, Tiger Woods, et al., mean that golf is a simplistic endeavor. No sport or game is merely hard (easy to lose) or easy (readily won). Instead, it's the game's complexity and the levels of skills needed to excel that make a sport genuinely challenging. If you frequently miss the target and fail to score, are you a failure or is the task truly difficult? Conversely, does a high rate of success imply that a target game is (too) easy? There are no simple answers to such questions, but they're interesting to ponder.

The Challenge of Playing

Most average people could play most of the games cited in this book. Obviously, they may not play at world-class level, but it's not too hard to throw darts or horseshoes. You could get the hang of billiards, lawn bowling, or shuffleboard if you tried. Most average people could likewise take part in most of the sports herein listed. Most of us can run (at least a short distance, if only slowly), many can swim, and we can toss and catch footballs. Dribbling, passing, and shooting basketballs on an elementary level is well within the grasp of "weekend warriors". Bowling is actively enjoyed by many people. Soccer balls are easy to kick to and from a partner. The majority of folks can lob a tennis ball back and forth over a net. Which sports, however, defy casual participation?

It may be fairly easy to swing a hockey stick and hit a puck, but could you do so while skating on ice, at high speed, changing directions fluently, with opponents flying at you with collision in mind? Imagine yourself stepping into a pair of skis or onto a snowboard to race down a mountain at speeds up to 90 mph, around gates, or launching yourself into aerial spins; you better have your health insurance premiums paid. Your life insurance better be in place before you take off on a 90-meter ski jump. Could you, with little or even a lot of preparation, pick up a long fiberglass rod, run to a plant box, and launch yourself high into the air as a pole vaulter? You could pick up a discus, shot, or hammer, but how far could you propel it without hurting yourself? Picture yourself a gymnast. As a guy, you're well over your head on the high bar, probably just hanging there and wishing against reality that you could spin around it, release into twists and somersaults before re-grasping the bar, and eventually soar into high-speed spins toward a balanced landing; before you actually try it, make sure your lawyer has an up-to-date copy of your will. As a gal, try some leaping, spinning, twisting runs across the floor exercise mat, move adroitly between the two uneven parallel bars, or climb onto the 4-inch balance beam for some flips and 360-degree turns. What would it take to rocket off a 3-meter springboard or leap off a 10-meter platform and squeeze in as many high-speed twists and somersaults as possible before stretching out at just the right split-second to knife vertically into a diving pool? Water is somewhat yielding, but landing flat on your back or belly from altitude takes your breath away. You'd probably look foolish trying to match the moves of synchronized swimmers. Project yourself onto a professional football field with the ball in your hands—could you run well enough to avoid being crunched by the big men in pursuit? Could you readily join a game of cricket or jai alai? It's easy to knock a croquet ball around a yard, but beware taking that up several notches to charge a polo ball on horseback. Some sports require strength, training, skill, timing, and daring far beyond what an average human being presently possesses.

Another part of the challenge of playing has to do with the distinction between individual and team sports. As an individual hitting a golf or tennis shot, self-responsibility rules. You accept your successes and mistakes, and continue to play on. Playing on a team, however, your actions are interdependent with those of others. Failure to execute a technique correctly upsets the apple cart; you risk being to blame for team losses. Your mates also depend on your contributions to victory. Hence, the interrelationships may make team participation more challenging than individual play.

Athleticism

It's also interesting to consider and debate which sport demands the best all-around athletic skills. The athletes in many of the aforementioned sports need to be endowed with multiple natural abilities, train hard to develop strength, agility, and endurance, and practice long hours daily to funnel their attributes into successful performance. Many people feel that basketball players best blend strength and agility, gross and fine motor coordination; they run, jump, pass, catch, dribble, and change direction, with power and coordination, pausing to take shots needing fine touch and eye-hand coordination. Playing football is athletically arduous on multiple levels; the top football players are physically and mentally agile as well as strong and fast. Gymnasts appear to be remarkably strong and fit; the best of them accomplish amazing feats. How about the athletes who engage in explicit feats of versatility, then? Might not decathletes, heptathletes, modern pentathletes, and triathletes be considered the most talented sports participants? Perhaps their multi-modal challenges are most demanding of all. Triathletes need awesome stamina along with well-developed musculature in order to swim, bike, and run up to Ironman distances (i.e., 2.4 miles, 112 miles, and 26.2 miles, respectively). The Olympic decathlon, by definition, requires well-developed skills in ten track & field events; women need similar attributes to accomplish the seven-event heptathlon. Modern pentathletes likewise need versatile, disparate skill sets. Who are some of the best all-around athletes competing today? Who are the best of all time? Are there high correlations among physical fitness, athletic acumen, and the qualities of target sports?

Human nature is fascinating. As if the many aforementioned sports are not challenging or engaging enough, people feel inspired to come up with variations on them. Is water polo too mundane or easy? Try playing a version of it in kayaks. Does basketball lack bounce? Play it while riding unicycles or wheelchairs. Is rifle target-shooting too sedate? Biathlon makes you cross-country ski from shot-to-shot. Blind people shoot darts with the aid of a string stretching from the bull's eye to the non-shooting hand for guidance. Chess boxing alternates intellectual with athletic demands, both at accelerated and intense levels. Golfers have taken their beloved activity to deserts, tundras, and ice fields.

So, again, which target game is truly most challenging? Because target games vary so much in their design, there is no way to do a scientific analysis (e.g., number of scores or errors per minute of play) to derive an answer. I've struggled at many of the aforementioned games; with a particularly long and intense history of frustration at golf, that sport gets a lot of my support. I've avoided sports too intimidating to attempt and can only imagine how hard it is to engage in diving, gymnastics, polo, pole vaulting, ski jumping, and other such challenges. As a spectator, I most appreciate the complexity of team strategy and interplay of college and NFL football; play-calling can be unpredictable, and no other sport affords the coaches and players the creativity to devise "trick" plays with which their opposition must contend. Close behind football in terms of viewing pleasure come college and NBA basketball, hockey, and major league baseball. Such team sports field a concatenation of players of different roles and positions who strive to achieve synergistic excellence. But it's player's choice. Take your pick and you'll be correct; after all, psychologists know that truth is about 90% perception and 10% reality. Whichever game gets your goat or floats your boat, that's the one that counts.

I'd like to hear from you, the reader. Shoot me an e-mail (drjimpsy@gmail.com) to let me know your vote. Feel free to give me a brief rationale for your opinion. As for me, my money's on writing as a challenging endeavor; not only do I not know whether or not this book will hit the mark, but I've now missed the wastebasket on the far side of my study with 41 of 67 crumpled pieces of rejected manuscript this month.

No matter how challenging a sport may be, the goal should be to play it. Yes, we "play" sports and games. We don't "work" them. Sure, we work at them, exercising and honing our skills in order to play better. It's healthiest to maintain the perspective that work and play overlap, whether the context is athletics or job, amateur or professional, serious or frivolous. According to Dr. Stuart Brown (2009), the characteristics that define play include inherent attraction (games are fun), freedom from time (athletes "in the zone" feel a distorted perception of the passage of time), diminished consciousness of self (less judgmental, more team-oriented), improvisational potential (moving and adapting on the spur of the moment, in response to fast-paced circumstances), and continuation desire (we want to play some more). Target games are meant to be enjoyed, win or lose, by spectators and participants alike.

REFERENCES

Anshel, Mark H. *Sport Psychology: From Theory to Practice.* Scottsdale, AZ: Gorsuch Scarisbrick, Publishers, 1994.

Bassham, Lanny. *With Winning in Mind: The Mental Management System.* Mental Management, 1995.

Ben-Shahar, Tal. *Happier: Learn the Secrets to Daily Joy and Lasting Fulfillment.* New York: McGraw-Hill, 2007.

Brodie, John & Houston, James D. *Open Field.* Boston: Houghton Mifflin Company, 1974.

Brown, Stuart, M.D. *Play: How It Shapes the Brain, Opens the Imagination, and Invigorates the Soul.* New York: Avery (Penguin), 2009.

Chopra, Deepak. *Golf for Enlightenment: The Seven Lessons for the Game of Life.* New York: Harmon Books, 2003.

Cox, Richard H. *Sport Psychology: Concepts and Applications.* Dubuque, IA: Wm. C. Brown Publishers, 1990.

Csikszentmihalyi, Mihaly. *Finding Flow: The Psychology of Engagement with Everyday Life.* New York: BasicBooks, 1997.

Diamant, Louis (Ed.). *Psychology of Sports, Exercise, and Fitness: Social and Personal Issues.* New York: Hemisphere Publishing Corporation, 1991.

Gallwey, W. Timothy. *The Inner Game of Golf.* New York: Random House, 1998.

Hebron, Mike. *The Art and Zen of Learning Golf.* Smithtown, NY: Rost Associates, 1990.

Hebron, Michael. *Golf Mind Golf Body Golf Swing.* Smithtown, NY: Rost Associates, 1993.

Herrigel, Eugen. *Zen in the Art of Archery.* New York: Vintage Books, 1999.

Karageorghis, Costas I., & Terry, Peter C. *Inside Sport Psychology.* Champaign, IL: Human Kinetics, 2011.

Knudson, R.R. & Ebert, P.K. (Eds.) *Sports Poems.* New York: Dell Publishing Co., 1971.

Kotler, Steven. *The Rise of Superman: Decoding the Science of Ultimate Human Performance.* New York: New Harvest, 2014.

Lardon, Michael, M.D. *Finding Your Zone: Ten Core Lessons for Achieving Peak Performance in Sports and Life.* New York: Perigee, 2008.

Lyubomirsky, Sonja. *The How of Happiness: A Scientific Approach to Getting the Life You Want.* New York: Penguin Press, 2008.

Mitchell, Bob. *The Tao of Sports.* Berkeley, CA: Frog, Ltd., 1997.

Parent, Dr. Joseph. *Zen Golf: Mastering the Mental Game.* New York, Doubleday, 2002.

Peck, M. Scott. *Golf and the Spirit: Lessons for the Journey.* New York: Three Rivers Press, 1999.

Ravizza, Ken. "Peak Experiences in Sport", presentations at the "Conference on Counseling Athletes". Springfield College, Springfield, MA, 1994 & 1996.

Rotella, Dr. Bob. *Putting Out of Your Mind.* New York: Simon & Schuster Source, 2001.

Townsend, Craig. *Mind Training for Swimmers: Everything You Need to Know.* Jamul, CA: Bellissima Publishing, LLC, 2005.

Weil, Andrew. *The Natural Mind: A New Way of Looking at Drugs and the Higher Consciousness.* Boston: Houghton Mifflin Company, 1973.

www.cbssports.com (online resource), 2016.

www.cricket-rules.com (online resource), 2016.

www.rio2016.com (online resource), 2016.

www.teamusa.org (online resource), 2016.

www.usoc.org (online resource), 2016.

www.wikipedia.org (online resource), 2016.

About the Author

• • •

JAMES WALLACE WAS BORN AND raised in Jamestown, NY, a region with changing seasons that afforded him easy access to both summer and winter sports. Family vacations expanded his immersion in water sports. He earned degrees from Dartmouth College and Cornell University before graduating from the University of Southern California with a doctorate in educational psychology. School psychology, teaching, and clinical practice have occupied most of his professional career, and he has augmented those pursuits with consultation with individual athletes and teams from Cornell and Colgate University. His professional writing, besides psychological evaluations, has included articles for *Aikido Today Magazine* and the *Seidokan Communicator*. He has also published a novel, *Holy Rollers*, featuring golf and aikido. He lives in Hamilton, NY, with his wife, Professor Ann Jane Tierney, while their two young adult daughters, Jasmine and Gemma Wallace, are forging careers in Virginia and Rhode Island, respectively.

www.ingramcontent.com/pod-product-compliance
Lightning Source LLC
Chambersburg PA
CBHW052031030426
42337CB00027B/4950